GLOUCESTER CATHEDRAL

A view of Gloucester from Clarke, *An Architectural History of Gloucester*, 1850.

Other books by David Verey

Shell Guides to Gloucestershire, Herefordshire, Wiltshire, Mid-Wales, and the Cotswold Section in the Shell Book of English Villages.

The Buildings of England: Gloucestershire, Vol. I The Cotswolds, Vol. II The Vale and the Forest of Dean. (1970)

Architecture in 'The Cotswolds, a New Study'. (1973)

Cotswold Churches. (1976)

The Work of G.F. Bodley in 'Seven Victorian Architects'. (1976)

The Diary of a Cotswold Parson. (1978)
   The Rev. F.E. Witts.

GLOUCESTER CATHEDRAL

David Verey
&
David Welander

ALAN SUTTON
1979

First published 1979 by

Alan Sutton Publishing Limited
17a Brunswick Road
Gloucester, GL1 1HG

ISBN 0 904387 40 2 case edition
ISBN 0 904387 34 8 soft cover

British Library Cataloguing in Publication Data

Verey, David
   Gloucester Cathedral.
   1. Gloucester Cathedral
   I.   Title II. Welander, David
   942.4'14   DA690.G5

Typesetting and origination by
Alan Sutton Publishing Limited
Set in Janson 11/13
Printed in Great Britain by
Redwood Burn Limited
Trowbridge & Esher

Contents

List of Illustrations

CATHEDRAL LIFE TODAY

The Dean of Gloucester

A cathedral is a place of life, which the building exists to interpret. The inspiration of its life is worship, shared by the clergy, choir and visitors welcomed from many lands; its words and music are of many periods from Solomon's Temple onwards, enriched by the brilliant developments of the last five centuries. The services include The Communion, the daily Prayers, and special services for vast numbers of people celebrating various events and activities. The choir entrance, crowned by the organ, welcomes visitors to share the worship within.

A cathedral is a great educational centre. Its School carries on an ancient tradition of teaching the young, particularly the choristers. The cathedral's educational work includes Music, Lectures, Discussions, Conferences, and other activities within the building, also a variety of outside activities. The Cathedral Bookstall contributes to education in an age when many people seldom visit a bookshop or even read a book.

Cathedrals are centres of pilgrimage. A pilgrimage is a journey with a purpose and a satisfying fulfilment. Past pilgrims visited sacred shrines — here, that of Edward II. Today pilgrims come to recover a sense of purpose in life; the value of this is great, when in a materialistic age life seems purposeless and dissatisfying for many. Cathedral Chaplains and Volunteer Guides give a personal welcome.

Cathedrals are today missionary centres, to a more widespread extent than ever before. Tourism has become a world movement of unprecedented proportions. Today over twenty million visitors enter the English cathedrals annually, and the task of interpreting the Faith to them, sharing the Christian belief in the holiness of the material creation through the sacred vessels in the Treasury, and proclaiming the worldwide mission of the Church to every area of life through the message of the bells, unlimited by words and international in its appeal, and through other means, is of incalculable and unlimited value.

Gilbert Thurlow

18th June 1979

Plate I. Osric, Prince of Mercia, founder of St. Peter's Abbey in AD. 681. The effigy is 16th century.

Chapter 1

HISTORY OF THE BUILDING

Gloucester Cathedral is one of the most beautiful buildings in England. Although it is not one of the biggest cathedrals, the Perpendicular eastern arm is incomparable.

The first monastic house built within the precincts of the present Cathedral was founded by Osric in AD681. He was the ruler of the Hwicce who had occupied much of Worcestershire and Gloucestershire east of the River Severn some fifty years earlier. In his day the whole area was part of the powerful Kingdom of Mercia, and he is described in charters as a *sub-regulus* or prince of Mercia.

Nothing remains of these early buildings, though Osric himself is commemorated by a shrine in the Cathedral in the founders place to the north of the high altar. This was put there at about the time of Abbot Parker, the last Abbot, who may have removed an effigy of Serlo, the first Norman Abbot from this position to a ledge on the south side of the presbytery.

The foundation of the monastery by Osric must have been a stimulus to the further development of the city. Timber buildings in the centre of the city have been dated by radio-carbon method to the 8th century. In 909 Ethelflaed, the daughter of Alfred, and her husband Ethelred, transferred the relics of St. Oswald to Gloucester, and founded a monastery called St. Oswald's Priory. The city at this time had a mint, and a royal palace at Kingsholm, and was evidently of particular significance to the rulers of Mercia. The Anglo-Saxon chronicle states that Ethelflaed and Ethelred were buried in St. Peter's Abbey; but the building of that date is not exactly on the site of our present Cathedral.

Aldred, Bishop of Worcester, began a new church in 1058, 'a little further from the place where it had stood, and nearer to the side of the city'. The original site seems to have been inside the Roman city wall;

Plate II. Large cylindrical Norman columns in the nave, from a drawing by John Carter, draughtsman to the Society of Antiquaries, + 1817.

but the Cathedral now stands fully over the North West corner of the Roman wall. In Saxon times the Roman walls still stood, and the East gate was still in use. A piece of Saxon sculpture was discovered some years ago in a garden near the Cathedral. It is a roundel of Christ, which according to the late Dame Joan Evans, 'sets Gloucestershire in the main current of European art somewhere about 950'.

In 1022 the Bishop of Worcester introduced the Benedictine rule to the monastery of St. Peter. However, according to William of Malmesbury, 'zeal and religion had grown cold many years before the coming of the Normans'. In 1072, when the Norman Serlo was appointed Abbot, the numbers were down to two monks and eight novices. The growth in wealth and importance of the religious houses in the first fifty years after the Conquest must have been remarkable; by 1100 Serlo had increased his numbers to 100 monks.

William the Conqueror kept Christmas in Gloucester in 1085, and this was the occasion when he ordered the compilation of the Domesday Book; but whether he was staying with the Abbot or at the Saxon Royal Palace at Kingsholm has not yet been established.

The foundation stone of the Abbey Church was laid on 29th June, 1089, and the building dedicated on 15th July, 1100. This was a considerable achievement; though it is probable that only the eastern arm was completed by this time. The nave westward of the first two bays was built after Serlo's death in 1104. Why was it, we wonder, that Serlo got Robert Bishop of Hereford to lay the foundation stone in 1089 and not his Diocesan Bishop Wulstan of Worcester? The Bishop of Hereford, a Frenchman from near Tournus, may have been involved in the choice of the large cylindrical columns for the nave, so like those at Tournus, and now fashionable in the West Country Abbeys such as Tewkesbury and Pershore, and Hereford Cathedral.

The Abbot who followed immediately after Serlo was called Peter and he reigned from 1104-1113, and it was he who presented to the Abbey the famous gold candlestick, made possibly by English gold-smiths in London, and elaborately decorated in the style of the time with fabulous little men and beasts. It is usually dated c. 1105, and was unfortunately early lost to Gloucester and was probably stolen because it was later given to the Cathedral at Le Mans in France. It remained there until the 19th century when it was acquired by the Victoria and

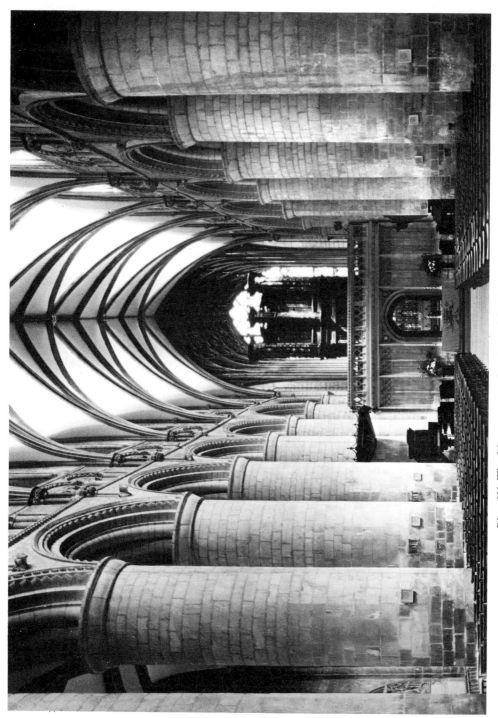

Plate III. The Norman nave showing calcination on the pillars.

Albert Museum.

The fire in 1122 must have been a disaster. In the nave there are signs of calcination on the pillars due to falling rafters. The fire risk would have been enormously reduced by having a stone vaulted roof; but the nave roof was of wood. The nave aisles retained their 11th century vaults, of which the northern one survives today. After such a disaster we would expect to find some account of repairs, but this is not so. By contrast, the repairs of a hundred years later are carefully recorded. The nave roof, however, must surely have been patched up for the time being. Gloucester's particular circumstances as well as those affecting the whole country provide ample reason for the long delay in repairing the ravages of the disaster of 1122.

To understand the circumstances of the Abbey in the 12th century, it must be kept in mind that it was situated next to a royal castle, one of the residences of whatever peripatetic monarch was in the ascendant, and was consequently in the centre of political strife. This was not the old palace at Kingsholm but a Norman castle built near the Abbey. It was the headquarters of Robert Earl of Gloucester, half-brother to the Empress Matilda, who when she was in power held her court there. On one occasion in 1142 she escaped from Oxford across the snow-bound Cotswolds to take refuge in Gloucester castle. That most interesting political character, Gilbert Foliot, Abbot from 1139-1148, was an open defender of the claims of Matilda to the English throne. Foliot was a severe and masterful man, who had been Prior of Cluny, and was destined to become Bishop of Hereford, and Bishop of London. He was Thomas á Becket's most formidable opponent. Abbot Hugh of Cluny, however, wrote of him as 'the mirror of religion and glory of the age, the luminary who shed lustre even on the great name of Cluny'.

In about 1170 the southern tower of the west front of the Abbey church collapsed. In 1194 the monks had to sell their silver plate to ransom King Richard I, an episode which rings a familiar note this century, and a third of their property was seized by King John in 1207; but Abbey and castle were joined together in the political scene when the loyal Barons assembled in the Abbey church to swear allegiance to the boy King Henry III, who was hurriedly crowned there, it is said with his mother's bracelet, in 1216.

Plate IV. The coronation of Henry III from a 19th century window by Clayton & Bell in the south aisle.

Plate V. Marginal drawing from 13th century copy of *Historia Regum Britanniae*.

The change of mood which came with the accession of the young King was electric. Hope and enterprise returned, exemplified in church life by an outburst of new building. This is the springtime of Early English architecture. At Gloucester the urge was felt, but compared with other Cathedrals there is little surviving to show for it. Ralph de Wylington in 1227 either refurnished the existing easternmost chapel at ground level, or extended it to form a new Lady Chapel. But nothing of his work has survived. The structure through which we now enter the Treasury however, belongs to this period, and could have been the entrance to the Lady Chapel, moved later to its present position in the North transept.

In 1242 the new vault over the nave was finished, and this is the most significant feature of the period left us. Anything else was swept away in the Perpendicular encasing of the presbytery and transepts and the rebuilding of the Lady Chapel in the fourteenth and fifteenth centuries.

In the margin of the verso of fo.82 of the Royal MS. 13A III in the British Museum, which is a 13th century copy of the *Historia Regum Britannie* of Geoffrey of Monmouth, there is a marginal drawing. This drawing was made in the mid 14th century and shows St. Peter's Abbey, Gloucester, from the west. We see a short stocky central tower, rather like the Norman tower at Tewkesbury, and this may well be Serlo's tower which survived the fire in 1122. It carries a very tall spire which seems to have a lead covering and must be the spire Elias is said to have built in 1222. The nave roof has a steep pitch and is the one finished in 1242. The west front has a high gable, with a tall west window with reticular tracery and this must be 14th century of which no written record survives. The south-west tower is shown with a little broach spire rebuilt c.1245. The north side of the west front is masked by a building which may be the 13th century part of the old Abbot's lodging (now Church House). This interesting doodle confirms our opinion that a very considerable amount of work took place at Gloucester especially within the precincts in the 13th century.

Contact between England and the Middle East existed in the early 14th century, owing to Crusades, pilgrimages, and travellers. The independent path taken by English art and architecture from the beginning of the 14th century has to be seen against the background of

Plate VI. The Decorated style of the west of England, encrusted with ballflower.

estrangement from France. There is no French parallel for the Kentish style which by 1300 was emerging in Canterbury. Several introductions of new forms into English architecture between 1290 and 1330 were unparalleled elsewhere such as the extensive use of the ogee curve and the complex geometrical interlaces, used at Canterbury, which are closely related to Persian patterns. The four-centred arch, never adopted in other parts of Europe suddenly appeared. The ogee curve, with its off-shoots in reticulated and flamboyant tracery were exploited for a time.

Before, however, the full effect of these innovations were felt at Gloucester, Abbot Thokey rebuilt the south aisle of the nave c.1319-1329, in the full-blown Decorated style of the West of England encrusted with ballflower. This was where the original Norman wall had probably been overturned by the unbalanced thrusts from the vaulting. Bowtells are treated as slender shafts, with their own capitals and hexagonal miniature bases and are the only details which look forward to the Perpendicular style. In every other respect this work is unrelated to London developments and also unrelated to work in Bristol less than thirty-five miles away. The master of this south aisle must have been brought from Hereford or somewhere else within the region of most intense addiction to ballflower, which is peculiar to the west front of Lichfield Cathedral, Wells Chapter House, Hereford central tower, c.1315-18, and Salisbury tower, 1320. Each window in the Gloucester aisle has 1,500 ballflowers, and the new vault has ribs decorated with ballflower in the three eastern bays. In local churches the ballflower is to be found particularly at Badgeworth where Gilbert de Clare, 10th Earl of Gloucester was possessed of the manor in 1314, and at Bishop's Cleeve.

On 20th September, 1327, King Edward II was horribly murdered in Berkeley Castle. The King's body had to be shown, and to appear as if he had died of natural causes. It is probable that Abbot John Thokey was ordered by the Court in London to bring the body in state to Gloucester, and at least some of the gear was sent down from London for the procession. The King's body was laid on the north side of the choir; but the funeral was delayed until 20th December, 1327 when Queen Isabella and her son the new King Edward III were present, at what was in fact a state funeral. It does not seem in these

Plate VII. The 'Pilgrims' Door', though mutilated by iconoclasts, is decorated on the inside and not on the outside, which indicates it was a way out of the transept into (according to W.H. St. John-Hope's plan) a sacrist's checker.

circumstances that Abbot Thokey was 'risking his life' by having the King buried in his Abbey. It is also assumed by some historians that immense sums in offerings at Edward II's tomb were provided by pilgrims which enabled the Abbey to undertake the work of transforming the Norman choir and presbytery into the Perpendicular master-piece we see today. This appears rather improbable, and the obvious source of money must have been the young King. The *Historia*, however, records that in Abbot Wigmore's time the offerings of the faithful were such that he rebuilt the south transept in six years (1329-35). The door in the south transept traditionally called 'The Pilgrims' Door' probably could not have been used for that purpose, and was an entrance from the transept into a sacristy rather than an entrance into the Abbey. Furthermore, later in the century the advowson of Holy Trinity church, which was situated near the congested way in to the Abbey from Westgate Street, was given to the Abbey 'in order to maintain the lights about the tomb of the King', which would hardly have been necessary had there been many pilgrims at that date.

The starting point of the Perpendicular style in England is the accession of Edward III, who did not assume full power until the autumn of 1330, and the specific marks of the new style appeared within the next year or so. The adoption of Perpendicular details in royal work provided the means of success. The royal taste set a fashion under the master masons to the crown and their pupils. The four-centred arch, never adopted in other parts of Europe, suddenly appeared then in the south transept of St. Peter's Abbey, Gloucester, where simple four-centred arches were used for the side window, 1331-35.

Perpendicular tracery first appeared in William Ramsey's cloisters at old St. Paul's, begun in 1332, and in the associated octagonal Chapter House. What passed into the general tradition of our later medieval architecture included the arch within a square surround, the four-centred arch, and the stiffened reticulations which were typical of the earliest Perpendicular tracery. Of these, the first two were derived from Persia, and the last from Cairo; in fact English architecture was partly conditioned by Edward III who had been tutored by the leading Orientalist of his day and by a mathematician

Plate VIII. The South Transept Window showing the first Perpendicular tracery. (The glass is 19th century by Hardman, depicting the life of St. Peter). The Historia states that in Abbot Wigmore's prelacy, because of his devotion towards King Edward, buried in the church, and because of the offerings of the faithful, he was able to carry out this work.

from whom he learnt geometry.

William Ramsey who was a freeman of good lineage and long descent in Norfolk had been in charge of St. Paul's from 1332-35 and his formulation of the Perpendicular style can be assigned to these years and preceded the appearance of any definitely Perpendicular detail at Gloucester Abbey. In spite of the parallel developments in the wall-panelling of Gloucester's south transept, the four-centred side windows have flowing tracery. Only the great South window has a minimal employment of the Perpendicular type detail, and the design of the latter is not earlier than c.1335. The detail is the fact that the mullions run straight into the arch in a vertical manner, and so this is the first extant Perpendicular window in the world; St. Paul's of course, no longer exists. Official work in progress at Gloucester Castle 1331-35 provided the obvious channel for information, and the inference must be that William Ramsey was in some way responsible for the window.

It was not merely that a set of new motifs however was put together in a manner aesthetically pleasing to the royal patron; but they were integrated with a whole philosophy of space and light, of unity of structure and composition which made Perpendicular a new art form. It is therefore fascinating to realise that Gloucester played such an important part in this new development. To the King this dark Norman choir must have appeared an unsuitable shrine for his father, and he must have welcomed the new ideas and techniques of his master masons, most especially of William Ramsey. Moreover, the *Historia* records the King's gifts worth £200 in Abbot Staunton's time (1337-51), together with a relic of the True Cross set in gold from his son the Black Prince, which was probably saleable, and relics set in gold from Queen Philippa. Queen Joan's gift of a great ruby could have been cashed straight away. The abbot was therefore able to pay for the transformation of the choir. The Perpendicular style was particularly adapted to English needs, both at Court and in the country. It lent itself to costly enrichment on the one hand, and to economical simplicity on the other. Its large windows glazed in light tones made the best of our habitually dull climate. Its shapes were mostly straight forward and could be made to appeal to the commonsense strain in the English character.

Plate IX. Abbot de Staunton (1337-51) out of the oblations presented at King Edward's tomb, caused the Perpendicular transformation of the Norman presbytery. The *Historia* records that King Edward III gave a golden ship which he redeemed for 100 l; the Black Prince gave a cross of gold; the Queen of Scots, a valuable necklace with a ruby, and Queen Philippa a heart and ear of gold, probably a holy man's relics set in gold.

Another name emerges at this time, that of John de Sponlee, who succeeded Ramsey in charge of the royal works at Windsor Castle from 1350 onwards. His name suggests he came from Spoonley near Winchcombe and probably therefore worked at Winchcombe Abbey. He was born c. 1310, trained between 1320 and 1335. John de Sponlee might well have been, as Howard Colvin indicates, the Master John the mason who carried out a survey of Gloucester Castle in 1336. Sponlee's shafting at Windsor, though nearly twenty years later, resembles the transept wall shafts at Gloucester which may indicate a possible involvement with work on the Abbey. He was pensioned by 1364. Another master mason was called Thomas of Gloucester. He was warden of the masons at Westminster Palace in 1354-5 and in 1356 the principal mason working on St. Stephen's Chapel.

As a model for the future of Perpendicular the eastern arm of Gloucester was not available until much more than half the 14th century had gone by, and it is therefore not extraordinary to find Perpendicular took time to catch on. Locally, on the Cotswolds emulation however lasted for a very long time, and the nave of Cirencester church, which clearly emulates the presbytery of Gloucester was not built till 1516-30.

John Morwent was abbot from 1421 (the year Henry V stayed in the abbey and attended Mass in the Abbot's chapel) till 1437. It was he who altered the west end of the nave. He also rebuilt the end two bays of the nave in Perpendicular style, and it is probable he had in mind to rebuild the whole of the nave which would, of course, have produced a more unified effect; but what a tragedy to have lost the vast Norman pillars. His Perpendicular architecture is elegant, however, particularly the South porch, and the West windows were extremely influential on the Cotswolds where they are to be found on a smaller scale in many churches like the west window at Withington.

Owing to the proximity of Bristol to Gloucester architectural historians have expected to find stylistic similarities; but according to Dr. John Harvey in his book 'The Perpendicular Style', there do not appear to be any. None of the traceries at Bristol resemble those at Gloucester, nor do the mouldings. In the 15th century the Gloucester style moves east towards Oxford or north into the West Midlands, whereas Bristol masons 'colonised' Somerset, Dorset and the South

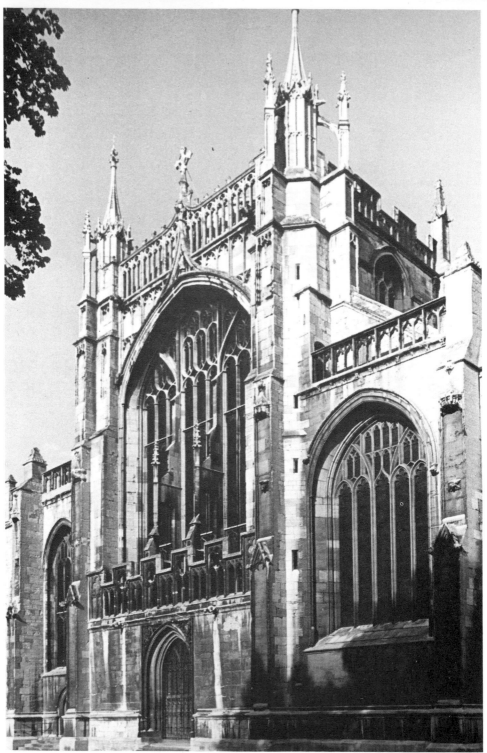

Plate X. Abbot Morwent's west front (1421-37).

Plate. XI. Northern hoodmould stop on Great West Window. Is it the Abbot?

Plate XII. The 15th century tower with its coronet of filigree openwork pinnacles and battlements.

West. We may also mention the almost universal employment of the diagonal buttress on Gloucestershire church towers, including the Cathedral and St. Nicholas church, in contrast to the general Bristol use of paired buttresses set back from the angle as in Somerset and the West of England.

The 15th century produced a wave of tower building. The tower at Gloucester (c. 1450) was based on the tower of Worcester Cathedral, which was built in 1357, but converted its turreted outline to diagonal buttressing, finishing with the famous Gloucester coronet of filigree openwork pinnacles and battlements, so largely copied on a reduced scale for parochial towers like that at Chipping Campden. The towers of Gloucester and Great Malvern Priory, roughly contemporary, are so alike that they have to be attributed to a single designer.

The last alteration to the Abbey, which was not finished till shortly before 1500, was the Lady Chapel. The reconstruction of Great Malvern Priory (c. 1430-60) nearly relates to the work at Gloucester, though the Lady Chapel adheres closely to the mouldings and traceries of the previous century. The 14th century vault was echoed on a smaller scale. Here and at Great Malvern the independent school of vaulting that had begun with the nave at Tewkesbury retained its individuality to the end, preserving as its hallmark a pair of subsidiary longitudinal ribs on each side of the main ridge. The East window has some glass, now very fragmentary, which was made at Great Malvern.

After the Dissolution of the monastery of St. Peter's, Gloucester, Henry VIII secured an Act of Parliament under which he created the See of Gloucester and the Abbey church became the Cathedral on 3rd September, 1541, 'considering the site of the late monastery in which the monument of our renowned ancestor the King of England is erected, is a very fit and proper place . . . '.

We see, once again, the results of the interment of Edward II at Gloucester. If this had not taken place it is quite likely St. Peter's Abbey might have been totally destroyed as were the neighbouring Abbeys of Winchcombe, Evesham, Hailes and Cirencester. The Abbot's Lodging became the Palace of the Bishop, the Prior's house became the Deanery and the cloister garth the private garden of the Dean. At times of religious fanaticism statues of saints were smashed

Plate XIII. Statue of Bishop Hooper in St. Mary's Square.

and reredoses hacked with axes as in the Lady Chapel. The monks' Refectory and Dormitory were pulled down. The reign of Bishop Hooper helps to account for the empty niches in the Cathedral.

After Queen Mary Tudor's accession he was deprived of his bishopric, imprisoned for a year, tried for heresy, and condemned to be burnt at the stake, which took place at Gloucester, outside St. Mary's Gate on 9th February, 1555. The Library has seven volumes of Hooper's works. He was not an original thinker, but absorbed the ideas of the more extreme Swiss reformers. He is often called the 'Father of English Puritanism'. He ordered all wooden screens to be removed in the Gloucester Diocese, thus causing untold damage to our artistic heritage.

At the time of the Civil War the Cathedral suffered less than might have been expected. It was, however, subsequently in grave danger of total destruction from the machinations of some people who are said to have 'agreed among themselves for their several proportions of the plunder expected out of it'. The Little Cloisters and the Lady Chapel were begun to be pulled down, and 'instruments and tackle provided for to take down the tower'; but in 1657 the church was made over by grant to the Mayor and burgesses at their request, and from this it is to be assumed that they wished to prevent it from possible ruin.

In 1679 a prebendary secured an order to destroy the old medieval glass in the West window of the tower. The apex of the vault under the crossing is some twenty feet higher than the roof of the nave and is taken up with a six-light window with glass which had escaped the iconoclasm of the 16th Century although it had a representation of the Trinity, similar to late 15th Century manuscripts. Prebendary Fowler described it himself. 'It was the old Popish picture of the Trinity. God the Father, an old man with a very long beard, the Son on a crucifix between his knees and the Holy Ghost a Dove with spread wings under his beard'. Fowler was shocked by this window and decided to get rid of it. He used the winding stair at the west end of the nave to get onto the nave roof. Walking along the parapet he could get within easy reach of the precious glass. He used a long pole. The subdean and others gazed upwards with horror as the fragments of medieval glass were scattered around them, and they saw framed in the empty tracery the fanatical face of the prebendary. Not even the Scotch soldiers who had

Plate XIV. Engraving by Thomas Bonnor published in 1796, showing William Kent's screen (1741) across the first bay of the Norman nave. His choir stalls are in the choir and there is no sign of a nave altar.

Plate XV. Engraving showing the choir with Georgian choir stalls and classical reredos. The pulpit is central.

Plate XVI. Drawing of the choir before Sir Gilbert Scott's restoration, showing the

done so much damage in the civil war, had been scandalised by the window. However, this wicked deed did the prebendary no harm, as he subsequently became Bishop of Gloucester; but that was after the revolution of 1688 which reversed the fortunes of High and Low.

High churchmen also had their day. Charles II did not forgive Gloucester for opposing his father in the civil war, in fact the siege may have cost Charles I his crown for in 1643 things looked well for the Royalists. Instead of marching directly to London after taking Exeter and Bristol the King made the fatal error of turning aside to take Gloucester. The siege lasted four weeks and the King failed to take the city. In 1662 Charles II ordered the destruction of the city walls. Robert Frampton, a Royalist who had fought for the King at Hambledon Hill was made Dean in 1673 and Bishop in 1680. He was devoted to the House of Stuart and a High Churchman. However, he refused the oath of allegiance to William and Mary, and was deprived of the bishopric.

In the 18th century, Bishop Benson (1734-52) spent vast sums of money on the Cathedral; but most of his innovations were removed in the 19th century when taste differed. Bishop Benson's period for art and architecture is now very much admired again, and we can appreciate his choir stalls and other furnishings in the nave today. William Kent, the most fashionable of architects, was employed to erect a screen in 1741. It is said that he would have liked to have fluted the Norman pillars; but that would have been a shocking deviation from historicism and good sense, and we can hardly believe it was considered very seriously.

Considering what Sir Gilbert Scott and other 19th century architects are accused of doing to our Cathedrals, Gloucester got off extremely lightly. Sir Gilbert Scott was here, but he seems to have behaved with great tact which in fact was very often the case, as indeed with the Wallers, a local dynasty of architects who looked after the Cathedral. Victorian architects, it must be remembered, were faced frequently with enormous difficulties in restoration work, by the neglect of the fabric in the previous century. It may indeed be to the credit of Bishop Benson and the like that Gloucester Cathedral was not falling down by the time the Victorians came on the scene, and did not require to be largely rebuilt.

Plate XVII. The bells were recast and retuned at the Whitechapel Bell Foundry, and a new treble and second were added to make a peal of twelve in 1979 under the auspices of the Dean.

A major scheme of repairs started in 1953, consisting of the reconstruction of the roofs of the nave, choir, north transept, and cloisters. The cloister roof incorporates pre-stressed and light-weight concrete for decking to carry the re-cast lead outer covering. The pre-stressed concrete roof to the South walk was probably the first time (1956) this material had been used in the repair of a medieval Cathedral in England. The architects were N.H. Waller and B.J. Ashwell.

Extensive work was carried out in the tower in 1977-79 under the direction of B.J. Ashwell. The floors of the ringing chamber and bell chamber were renewed, and a new bell frame in iroko wood installed, replacing the old oak frame dated 1632. Great Peter, England's only remaining medieval Bourdon bell, was retuned and given a new headstock to enable it to be swung again having been fixed in its frame since 1878. The remaining bells in the chamber above were either recast or retuned at the Whitechapel Bell Foundry and a new treble and second were added to make a peal of twelve.

Plate XVIII. The view of the Cathedral from College Green gives the impression that it is a Perpendicular building, but closer inspection reveals its Norman bones. The Norman turrets of the South Transept can be seen on the right. When the first Perpendicular window was placed between the turrets, Norman chevrons in single stones were reset round its outside, together with groups of additional 14th century chevrons, two or three to a single stone.

Chapter 2

LOOKING AROUND OUTSIDE

Generally, the Cathedral is built of pale cream Cotswold stone from Painswick, but the exposed battlements and pinnacles as well as the bottom courses of the walls are mostly of stone from Minchinhampton.

The first view of the Cathedral, as it opens before one's eyes on entering College Green from College Street, gives the impression that it is a Perpendicular building. Closer inspection reveals its Norman bones in the rounded two-storey ambulatory with radiating chapels, and in the gabled ends of the transepts flanked in both cases by sturdy Norman turrets. The windows of the crypt, the ambulatory, and the ambulatory gallery also largely retain their round-headed Norman openings, though many are filled with later tracery. The radiating chapels are polygonal in plan, and east of either transept is a chapel too, of an oddly indistinct, rounded shape. Moreover, at gallery level are two small bridges which have blank Norman arcading with zigzag. These are reset Norman work.

Such details, however, cannot at first be apparent to the eye, overwhelmed as it must be by the immense mid 15th century Perpendicular **Tower** which soars 225ft., piercing the sky with its celebrated coronet of open parapet and airy pinnacles, and patterned all over with louvred openings and tiers of blank arcading. The admirable effects of light and shade are produced by the bold projection of the diagonal buttresses, and the deep recessing of the windows and mouldings, and culminate in the openwork pinnacles at the top, each like the fantastic model of a church tower, and the openwork parapet and battlements.

Plate XIX. Drawing by John Carter of the south side of the Cathedral showing the first Perpendicular window tracery in the South Transept.

Plate XX. Drawing by John Carter of a south aisle window, and (on left) the entrance to the slype passage.

Plate XXI. Engraving by Thomas Bonnor of the south side of the Cathedral in 1797 showing the 18th century appearance of the Deanery on the left, and the south porch without J.F. Redfern's statues.

Having returned to earth as it were, one finds oneself facing the **South Porch,** which is the main entrance to the Cathedral. This, like the rather similar porch at Northleach, was built c. 1420, but the niches are now filled with 19th century figures by Redfern. Inside it is beautiful with stone panelling and a lierne-vault, and the inner doors have Norman hinge-work with trident-shaped iron strengtheners, thought to have been moved from the original Norman West door and adapted to fit the pointed doorway. The porch has an open parapet and pinnacles like the tower in miniature.

The **South Aisle** is buttressed, and some of the niches retain sculpture, notably Prince Osric at the east end, all much worn by the weather and contrasting, though recently cleaned, with the over-restoration of the Porch. All the windows, which are early 14th century, are profusely ornamented with thousands of ballflower. (This represents thc only large extent of the high Decorated style of the West Country in the Cathedral.) Ogee arches are entirely absent, a note-worthy sign of conservatism. The tracery in each window has a horizontal emphasis, and gives the impression of a large butterfly. There are seven bays altogether, and the easternmost window, although also decorated with ballflower, is similar to the Perpendicular of the South transept. The clerestory windows above have ogee shapes in the tracery and together with an embattled parapet date from the 15th century; but between the windows are the shallow Norman buttresses with chevron at the angles, which stop two bays from the west front. These two bays are Perpendicular, as the **West End** was rebuilt in c.1421 by Abbot Morwent. It has two doorways, the main one set with its surrounding masonry in front of the plane of the nine-light west window. The projecting wall ends in a pierced parapet. Against the west window stand two thin flying buttresses, and left and right are two dainty turrets with flying buttresses. The second door enters the north aisle and is called The Dean's door.

The Norman **Transept Fronts** have turrets ornamented with arcading in two tiers (one with intersecting arches, the other with zigzag), and in the gable is a group of stepped, lancet-shaped, round-headed blank arches profusely provided with zigzag. Below, in spite of the Perpendicular remodelling, are long vertical lines of chevron. These seem to be in situ, whereas the chevron round the great south

Plate XXII. The Lady Chapel is almost detached from the Great East Window, the outer hoodmould of which turns into ogee shape and rises to the perforated parapet of the gable.

window cannot be. Below this is the earliest extant Perpendicular window, dating from c.1335. It is awkward as regards tracery, but a turning-point in the history of English architecture, for here the mullion strikes the main arch vertically for the first time, a sign that the King's master mason has arrived. The transept windows to the west must have been designed first, for in their tracery simple ogee motifs suffice, whereas the south window has strictly Perpendicular panel tracery, with supermullions and vertical hexagons.

In the **Ambulatory Tribune,** or gallery, a Decorated window with ballflower ornament is matched by a similar window in nearly the same position on the north. If the south aisle windows are c.1318, these, because they use ogees as well as ballflower, may be dated c.1325-30.

Perhaps the *tour de force* of the whole edifice is the **East Window** with its fourteen lights, its canted side wings making the composition 4-6-4, with three transoms in the wings and five in the centre. The grid-frame dictated by the foundations in the crypt, gives strength against wind pressures. At its date, this was the largest window in the world. The outer hood-mould turns into ogee shape and rises to the perforated parapet of the gable, flanked either side by pierced pinnacles. In order to give full light to the window, the **Lady Chapel** is almost detached. This, the last alteration to the monastery, was not finished till shortly before 1500. Though about a hundred years later than the choir, the Lady Chapel is stylistically indistinguishable. The tracery patterns are pretty well the same. The east window has nine lights and three transoms, and an openwork parapet finishes the composition. Two identical chantry chapels project north and south, their fenestration in two tiers. On the north side of the Cathedral the library is seen to bend round the north chapel of the transept where it was enlarged in the 14th century, and next to it is the large Perpendicular window of the Chapter House. Beyond this lie the cloisters.

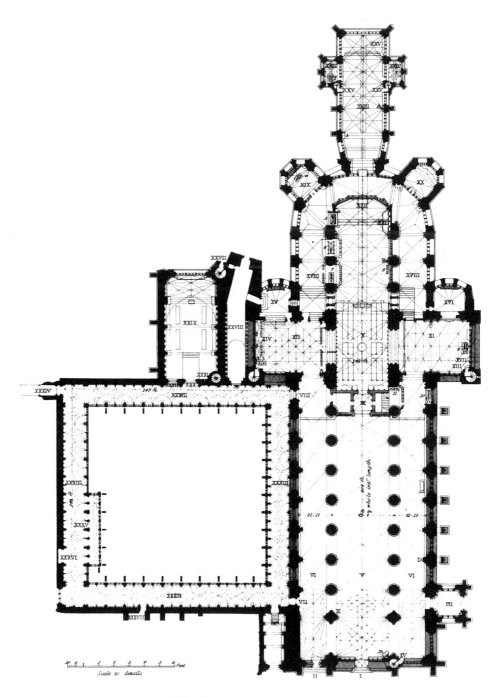

Plate XXIII. Plan of the interior.

Chapter 3

EXPLORING INSIDE

The **Nave** is dominated by the huge cylindrical Norman columns of the arcades, which have narrow, round, convex capitals similar to those at Tewkesbury (consecrated 1121) and probably a regional fashion. Seven bays with round Norman arches of three contrasting orders, a pair of strong soffit rolls, a straight edge, and chevron at right angles to the wall; the arches are not wide, as the massive columns are comparatively close together. Above this is a narrow band of triforium on a string-course with chevron. The triforium is remarkably small (cf. Tewkesbury) and has two twin openings with short columnar piers and responds, scallop capitals, and chevron at right angles to the wall. The Norman clerestory seems to have had chevron set vertically, but only traces of this work remain. Springing from the line of the triforium is the Early English rib-vault added in 1242, an elegant and graceful hat that hardly fits the rugged face below.

The **Vault** can be criticised as being too low. The probable reason for this is that much of the old Norman roof would have still been in existence in 1235, and to keep the weather out they built below it, a bay or two at a time. The first thing the builders had to do was to alter the walls of the Norman clerestory in order to reduce their height because the new vault would be built against these walls, and the timber roof would eventually rest upon the wall-plate.

It is supposed that the masons began from the west end, and as they approached the crossing they realised they had not calculated the spaces correctly. The statement in the *Historia* appears to say the monks finished the work themselves without the assistance of the craftsmen they had at the beginning. As we look at the vault today,

Plate XXIV. The nave vault as it was in 1242 except for the two western bays altered by Abbot Morwent.

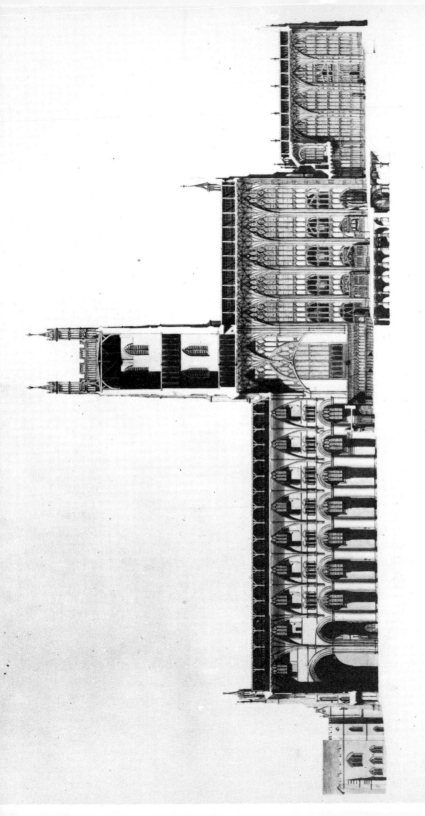

Plate XXV. John Carter's section through the Cathedral which does not clearly show the difference in the two eastern bays of the nave vault. The difference could be to do with the fact that in monastic times they would have been behind the nave altar and screen. At Tewkesbury the corresponding two eastern bays are markedly different to the rest of the nave.

except for the two West bays altered later, the 13th century vault remains as it was in 1242. The first four of the remaining bays are identical in design, the last two are different. In the four bays the vault springs from a cluster of short Purbeck marble shafts standing on the floor of the triforium stage, which is divided from the arcade below by a string course with a chevron moulding. Below this are extension vaulting shafts which descend between the arches of the arcade and end in corbel heads. In the two eastern bays there are no clusters of Purbeck marble shafts, and the springing of the vault is dropped several feet down to the level of the triforium floor. At the same position the ridge member of the vault, which from the west has been of fairly broad proportions, is now greatly diminished in width.

There is a steady rise in the apex of the vault from west to east amounting to eighteen inches in all and three inches in the two East bays. Perhaps it was at this point that the monks were parted with their master mason, who may have left to work for the King, and had to finish the job as best they could, by stilting the vault from a lower position in order to make up the error. This was a clever solution to the problem; but we must admit that the somewhat unhappy relationship between the vault, beautiful though it is in itself, and the Norman work below, does provide aesthetic grounds for criticism.

In the early 15th century the Norman west end of the **Nave,** and the two most westerly bays, were altered in the Perpendicular style and given lierne-vaulting. The longitudinal ridge-rib has two parallel subsidiaries left and right, exactly as in the choir vault. The north aisle retains its Norman rib-vault with ribs of two rolls and a spur between, but the south aisle was remodelled c. 1318 and has a vault of that period with ribs decorated with ballflower in the three east bays.

The most easterly bay of the Norman nave is blocked with the pulpitum and organ chambers. In monastic times there was a second screen in line with the present nave altar, and there were altars in the two aisles, so that everything east of this line was, in the peculiarly English fashion, completely screened off from the nave. The rather dull Perpendicular panelling on the existing stone screen is 19th century. On its south side is the Chapel of the Salutation of Mary, 15th century Perpendicular, commonly known as the Seabroke Chapel. To the east, the Chapel of St. John, with a Late. Perpendicular stone

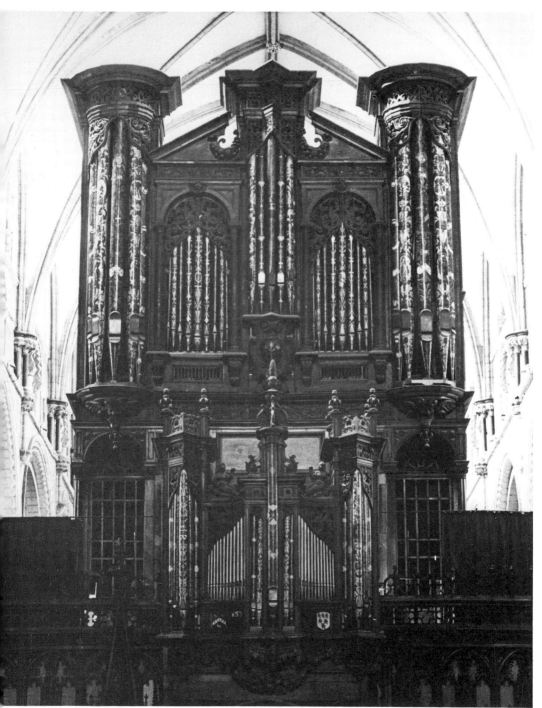

Plate XXVI. Thomas Harris's Organ has a fine case of 1665.

XXVII. Detail of the Organ showing initial C for Charles II.

reredos, restored in 1964 by Stephen Dykes Bower. This chapel is against the back of the choir stalls and is protected on the south by a fine wooden parclose screen.

The early 18th century Choir Stalls and Bishop's Throne in the Nave were turned out of the choir in the 19th century by Sir George Gilbert Scott. The Pulpit is 17th century, with stairs and sounding board designed by Stephen Dykes Bower c.1946: Nave Altar also by Dykes Bower. Lectern, first half of the 17th century; wood. The nave lacks a font. A font designed by Scott in 1873 carved in the Romanesque style in granite was removed some years ago to the crypt. Thomas Harris's Organ (rebuilt in 1920) has a fine case of 1665. The pipes were painted by Campion, a local man, in heraldic designs; on the nave side initials of Charles II. On the south of the organ chamber, above the Seabroke chapel is some Elizabethan wood panelling, similar to that in the Laud Room of the Old Deanery.

The **South Transept** (where, as has already been noted, the Perpendicular style was first developed in the South window, and four-centred arches were used in the side windows, between 1331 and 1335) is Norman with a skin of Perpendicular panelling crossed by the great flying buttresses of the tower. The slight movement of the tower southwards must have caused concern. On the north east corner the vertical of the Perpendicular panelling has had to be rebated into the tower in order to keep truly vertical, and the huge flying buttresses, which penetrate the rectilinear system, must have been considered a necessity. The vault of the transept is a complicated and early example of a lierne-vault, without the benefit of any boss to cover up the sometimes inexact meetings. It shows a total ignorance of what was happening in London, and also ignorance of the Bristol style of net-vaulting. It is yet a triumph of solid geometry by the master who designed it.

Generally, however, the work in the south transept is made up of several disparate parts: the side windows, the wall panelling, the south window, and the vault. As an innovating treatment the design is of great interest, but the aesthetic impression is disappointing. We can admire, however, the displays of virtuosity, the four-centred arches, the ogee shapes, the moon-like cusps, the hexagonal bases to the tall bowtells, the frilly tops of the twin entrances to crypt and ambulatory

Plate XXVIII. We can admire the moon-like cusps and frilly tops of the twin entrances to ambulatory and crypt, and the figures set in trefoils above them.

Plate XXIX. Engraving of 1828 showing the entrance to the crypt.

Plate XXX. Bracket of the master mason of the South Transept.

and the figures set in trefoils above them which are carved detached from the wall.

On the east side is the Chapel of St. Andrew. This, too, is Norman with an irregularly rounded or three-sided apse. The Wall Paintings, representing incidents in the life of the saint, and other decoration, are by Thomas Gambier-Parry, 1866-68. The Perpendicular stone reredos with figures was restored in the 19th century and redecorated recently in memory of Bishop Guy. On the left of the entrance to the chapel is a carved stone bracket with dowel holes for the image which stood on top of it. It is L-shaped, in other words the shape of the medieval equivalent of the architect's T square, and so the bracket and the image for which it was put up may be a gift of the master mason. The figures below look convincing for that role, and there is a little lierne-vaulting on the underside of the bracket. The master of the transept is apparently looking up as one of his masons is falling from the vault.

The small South doorway, with side pieces like the arms of a throne, may be the entrance to a no-longer existing sacristy. There is no enrichment on the other side. Another doorway in this wall is blocked up.

In spite of the common factors between the south transept and the work which followed in the choir and presbytery there seems to have been a change of master mason. Could it be that the King's interest was aroused, Ramsey arrived, finished off the transept and then designed the choir and presbytery, which shows such close stylistic resemblance to the bay designs of St. Paul's Chapter House? The actual mouldings also indicate Ramsey's direct influence, and the window tracery is completely Perpendicular in character. These plans could all have been made before the death of Abbot Wigmore on 28th February 1337. The dates within which this whole work was designed and executed cannot be made more precise than the thirty years between 1337 and 1367, and this includes the year of the Black Death in 1349 in which about one third of the total population died, including Ramsey — who died on June 3rd. It used to be said that Perpendicular was an economy-style, produced in the aftermath of the Black Death when labour was dear and simplification of detail was necessary. This is disproved by the fact that the style already existed before the Black Death, both here and in London.

Plate XXXI. The entrance into the South Transept from the nave aisle.

Plate XXXII. Stone ogee arches in mid-air from which rise the seven ribs of the vault. The design emphasises the spatial unity with the choir and isoletes the transepts.

The Norman **Crossing** survives, though the west and east piers
have been altered. To the north and south the piers have twin responds. The masons of the 14th and 15th centuries did a marvellous
conversion of the upper parts. It is as well to remember that what a
building looked like was always as important to the medieval mason as
was structure and function. In order to vault the crossing in his lierne
manner, the master mason needed in theory points of support in the
middle of the crossing arches; but this cannot have been so in fact, for
he threw across the wide space arches so flat and so thin that they are
hardly capable of carrying any weight, and look as if they were
borrowed from a timber structure. On the not very pronounced apexes
of each of them he placed a vertical mullion accompanied on both sides
by counter-curves. The result is a stone ogee arch in mid-air from
which rise the seven ribs of the vault. This is a very original stylistic
conceit which by contrast emphasises the spatial unity with the choir
and isolates the transepts. The twin Norman respond mouldings at the
crossing were joined together, and from them rise the mouldings of the
mid 14th century tower arches.

An examination of the **East End** must begin below ground in the
Crypt; for the crypt was naturally the part with which building began,
i.e. it dates from 1089 and the following years. The crypt represents
the Norman plan above, with ambulatory and three radiating chapels.
England has six such crypts: Canterbury Cathedral; St. Augustine,
Canterbury; Winchester; Worcester; Rochester; and Gloucester. At
Worcester the centre part is four-naved; at Canterbury, in both
buildings, and at Gloucester, three-naved. The Gloucester centre has
columns with typical late 11th century volute capitals and groin-vaults.
The wall-shafts have equally typical late 11th century two-scalloped
capitals. In the ambulatory and the chapels are elements of the same
date, but very shortly after completion of the ambulatory the masons
must have realised that for their superstructure, with the sturdy round
piers of which more will be said presently, the ambulatory needed
strengthening. So rounded responds were set below the upper piers,
and strong, elementary ribs were inserted, either of plain rectangular
section or of one broad half-roll with two smaller quarter-hollows.
There is no decoration, except somewhat later pieces of blank arcading
in the south east and east chapels and some chevron at right angles to

Plate XXXIII. The Crypt, dating from 1089.

Plate XXXIV. Half-tunnel vaults in the Norman tribune with radiating chapel.

Plate XXXV. Norman presbytery masked by Perpendicular panelling begun after 1337.

Plate XXXVI. The vault with three longitudinal ridge-ribs and such a multiplication of liernes and tiercerons that it looks like a net.

the wall in the north east chapel and the ribs of the vault in the ambulatory nearby.

What the Norman **Choir** and **Presbytery** looked like, one can see better in the ambulatory than in the centre. The elevational system was completely different from that later adopted in the nave, and in this respect it differs from Tewkesbury. It is the normal Norman system of arcade and gallery, both here with strong round piers. The piers have the same convex minimal capital bands as later in the nave. The transverse arches are of plain rectangular section. The wall shafts have single-scallop capitals, and the vaults are groined. All this is still as in the crypt. The entries from the transept to the ambulatory have twin shafts. On the gallery the extremely interesting feature is the half-tunnel vaults, a feature rare in England but frequent in France ever since Tournus of about the year 1000. The radiating chapels have tunnel-vaults, but the Norman east chapel is of course replaced by the present Lady Chapel.

The guiding principle of the masons working on the choir and presbytery in the 14th century was to create a unification of the whole space, and how well they succeeded. In the centre the Norman work is entirely masked by the Perpendicular panelling begun after 1337. The Norman piers have been partly sliced off to make room for the Perpendicular shafts, which are anchored at the ground and gallery stage. From the floor by the choir stalls to the apex of the vault is about 92ft. The vault with its longitudinal ridge-rib is accompanied by two parallel ribs left and right — a motif invented here and, as we shall see, taken over in the north transept (and the west bays of the nave). The vault shows such a multiplication of liernes and tiercerons that it is to be considered more textural than structural. Basically it is a double quadripartite vault. As the points of crossing increase, so do the bosses. They intensify the impression of texture, appearing to be heads of nails fixing a net to the vault.

The vault was painted by Clayton and Bell c.1895. At the east end, centrally over the high altar, is a figure of Christ in Glory, and on the surrounding bosses angels playing musical instruments, and carrying Passion emblems, an idea taken from the slightly earlier series at Tewkesbury, and much finer. The vertical lines of the shafts on the walls are nowhere cut by the horizontals, nor are the main mullions of

Plate XXXVII. At the east end, centrally over the High Altar, is the figure of Christ in Glory.

Plate XXXVIII. On the surrounding bosses angels playing musical instruments and carrying Passion emblems.

Plate XXXIX. Carter's drawing of the East Window: like a 'glass wall'.

the East Window, so that the impression of soaring height is intensified. The East Window is canted to position the foundations of the main mullions on the crypt walls below. A spin-off advantage was that it became canted against wind pressure; all the same the east bay of the vault looks as if it is held up by a glass wall. The panelling runs blank over Norman wall surfaces, and open where there were Norman openings. The Gloucester feature of close cusping is noticeable in the ogee arches of the stone panelling.

The Chronicle says it was not until the time of Abbot de Horton (or Houghton), 1351-77, that the work of the presbytery with the high altar and second half of the stalls, was undertaken. Against this, the heraldry in the East Window shows it to be largely a memorial to those who fought at Crecy in 1346. If the date of the presbytery, clerestory and east window are on the other hand as late as John Harvey says, it tends to identify the master of the great east window (and the east cloister as well) hypothetically with Thomas of Cambridge. But to arrive at this hypothesis we must later consider the Cloisters.

The **Choir Stalls** of c. 1350, are very perfect, with their three-dimensional ogee-arched canopies and a wonderful series of fifty-eight misericords of which fourteen were made when the choir was restored by Scott in 1873. Some of the subjects are copied from those at Worcester. The carvings mostly consist of folk-tales, domestic scenes, and fabulous monsters rather than religious subjects. One depicts, for example, 'playing at ball', another Knights jousting, Reynard the fox, bear baiting, hawking, a mermaid, a pelican in its piety, and an elephant complete with howdah, and provided with hairy hoofs like a carthorse and with a horse's tail. The tip-up seats allowed the monks to get support when standing for very long services. It is supposed that the carving was left to the carpenter's invention, and no one saw them thereafter except the monks. Generally the interest is more historical than aesthetic, giving insight into the folk mind and into medieval humour which was coarse rather than keen. The sub-stalls of the 19th century by Sir Gilbert Scott, are very fine, with splendidly carved ends and finials. The choir stalls occupy the whole space of the crossing. Part of a 13th century stall can be seen behind that of the vice-dean, on the north of the opening under the organ. There are contemporary paintings of Reynard the fox on the back of the stalls on the

Plate XLI. Three-dimensional ogee-arched canopies.

north side. The floor is covered in 19th century encaustic tiles and marble slabs.

The sanctuary retains much of Abbot Seabroke's tiled pavement laid down in 1455 in front of the high altar. The **High Altar** itself, and the recently painted reredos were designed by Sir George Gilbert Scott in 1873, with realistic groups of figures carved by Redfern. The polychroming of the figures has pulled the whole composition together, with its new Cross and Candlesticks by Stephen Dykes Bower. The three upper turrets have statues of angels under the canopies. Everywhere Scott has seen to it that the cusping is of the Gloucester variety, echoing King Edward II's tomb. The restored or recarved quadruple sedilia are in detail much more commonplace, though the embattled parapet has three delightful cherubs sitting casually upon it and playing musical instruments.

The brass Lectern is c. 1866 and is a splendid example of Victorian craftsmanship, with eagle and dragon, designed by J.F. Bentley. There are many modern gifts to the Cathedral which all beautify the building. The Embroidery and Needlework Guilds of the Friends of the Cathedral have made the cushions in the monks' stalls. At the back of the Bishop's Throne and the Mayor's stall there is a wooden tablet which tells us what each cushion represents. Among the High Altar frontals is one designed by L.C. Evetts. In 1956 the choir was relit to the design of Mr. Waldran by the G.E.C. Research Laboratories. The light fittings were designed by Bernard Ashwell, and the Paschal Candlestick (1973) by Basil Comely. The latter was made in the Cathedral workshop; it is dressed with flowers between Easter and Whitsun.

Returning to the south ambulatory, before coming to the Lady Chapel we pass a 15th century cope chest, and St. Stephen's Chapel. The chapel has a stone Perpendicular screen and windows, and a panelled reredos.

The **Lady Chapel** is entered under the bridge which carries a small chapel and the passage running outside the window. The apse seems to have been three-sided rather than absolutely round. The chapel was finished c. 1500 with a lierne-vault, and an east window very similar in design to that of the choir sanctuary, though nearly a hundred and fifty years later. On the north and south sides are Chantry Chapels with fan-

Plate XLII. The Victorian reredos by Sir Gilbert Scott which was painted c.1890, J.F Redfern's figures being left unpainted; these were painted in c.1969.

Plate XLIII. The Lady Chapel was the last alteration to the abbey though it adheres closely to the mouldings and traceries of the previous century.

Plate XLIV. The Lady Chapel finished c.1499 with a lierne vault and three parallel ridge-ribs. Chantry chapel on north has effigy of Bishop Goldsborough + 1604.

Plate XLV. Dean Laud's communion rails.

vaults ingeniously adapted to an oblong plan. They support singing galleries which are held up by flying ogee arches across the open-panelled stone screens. In the South Chapel is a reredos with embroidery designed by W.H.R. Blacking. The sanctuary floor, separated by Dean Laud's communion rails (square, tapering balusters), has medieval tiles. The reredos is late 15th century, but much mutilated. It is unusual in preserving contemporary graffiti or scribbled memoranda of the names of the saints whose statues once adorned it. The restored triple sedilia are contemporary. We know the Lady Chapel was built under Abbots Hanley and Farley (Richard Hanley, 1457-72, and William Farley, 1472-99).

Returning to the **North Ambulatory,** the Chapel of St. Edmund and St. Edward on the right hand side is dedicated as a War Memorial. It was formerly known as Boteler's Chapel, after Abbot Boteler (1437-1450). It is also separated from the ambulatory by a Perpendicular screen. The 15th century Perpendicular reredos is mutilated; it was coloured. The stone altar has been restored. The floor is covered with rather worn medieval tiles. Opposite, on the south side of the ambulatory is the 16th century tomb of Osric, the founder on the first monastic house on this site in 681. Further along is the tomb of Edward II murdered at Berkeley Castle in 1327. And still further west the cenataph of Abbot Parker, the last Abbot of St. Peter, Gloucester who was buried elsewhere. These memorials are described in detail later.

By the Perpendicular screen between the **North Transept** and the north ambulatory is a stone reading desk. This was the entrance for the monks coming from the cloister into the choir, and the reading desk could well have been useful for superintendence. The screen openings are similar to those on the south side in the same position. On the east side of the north transept is the Chapel of St. Paul, furnished in 1928. The reredos is 19th century. The date of the chapel is the same as that of the ambulatory — see the twin responds with single-scallop capitals and the groin-vault. It looks as if the work of 1089-c. 1100 went as far as the lower parts of the transepts. In their upper parts chevron has arrived, on the outside, as it has also in the nave.

The North Transept, like the one on the south side was given a Perpendicular veneer, but at a later date — between 1368 and 1373. The lierne-vaulting is also later and more accomplished. The longi-

Plate XLVI. In the Perpendicular screen between the north transept and the north ambulatory is a stone reading desk perhaps useful for superintendence.

Plate XLVII. Engraving of 1796 of the north transept showing cells for punishment in what is now the entrance to the Treasury.

Plate XLVIII. The 13th century entrance to the Treasury.

tudinal ridge-rib has a parallel rib either side, as in the choir, and the intersections of the ribs are covered by bosses. The entrance to the Treasury, given by the Goldsmiths Company in 1977, is through the north wall of the North transept so visitors pass through the Early English screen which is not in situ and is probably part of the narthex of the Early English Lady Chapel, which was finished in 1227. It probably dates from c. 1230-40. It is profusely enriched with Purbeck marble shafts, the only place in the Cathedral apart from the nave vault where this was done. The elevation is tripartite with window-like openings left and right. The shaft capitals are of the most dramatic stiff-leaf types. The centre bay has the doorway with a trefoiled head set under a pointed gable, blank trefoils, and an eight-cornered star whose diagonal corners are pointed-trefoiled. The side arches have stiff-leaf covering the spandrels. Inside are three little rib-vaults with fillets on the ribs.

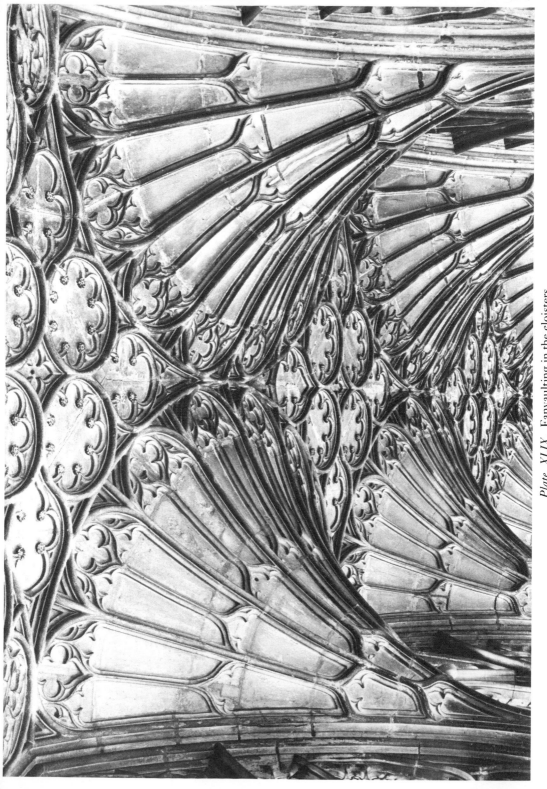

Plate. XLIX. Fanvaulting in the cloisters.

Chapter 4

DISCOVERING THE MONASTIC PAST

The **East Walk of the Cloisters** has the earliest fan-vaulting known; the date is some time after 1351 and before 1377. There is a close link between the Hereford chapter house (1364-70, only known to us from slight fragments and from a drawing of 1721) with its fan-vault on a grand scale and the smaller fan-vaults and traceries of the east cloister at Gloucester. At Hereford the construction was undertaken by Thomas de Cantebrugge, mason and citizen of Hereford, from 1365-71. He originated probably at Cambridge near Gloucester. The six bays of the east cloister from the transept to the door of the chapter house were built under Abbot Horton but this merely fixes the date between 1351 and 1377. In spite of their smaller scale the traceries and fan-vaults of the cloister correspond so exactly with the style and details used at Hereford there can be no doubt the designer was one and the same man. As a working hypothesis it is suggested that Thomas of Cambridge was in charge at Gloucester for some time before 1364, and built the early bays of the east walk, that he then left to take on the important contract at Hereford and set himself up there by investing in the freedom of the city, and that Robert Lesyngham was thereupon appointed master mason at Gloucester. In this case Lesyngham would be the designer of the North transept and of the remainder of the cloisters. There is a subtle distinction between the east walk of the cloisters and the other three walks not begun until 1381, the difference between the work of two architects Cambridge and Lesyngham. The style of the North transept (1368-73) seems closer to the later walks of the cloisters.

The panelling of the east walk and its corresponding windows is

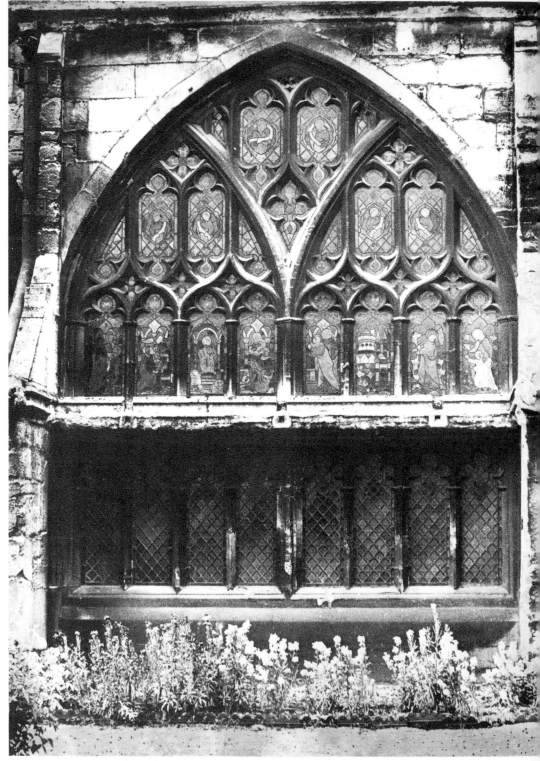

Plate L. Window in East walk of the Cloisters with interlacing ogee archlets.

Plate LI. Window in South walk with lower windows for carrels, where the monks read and wrote.

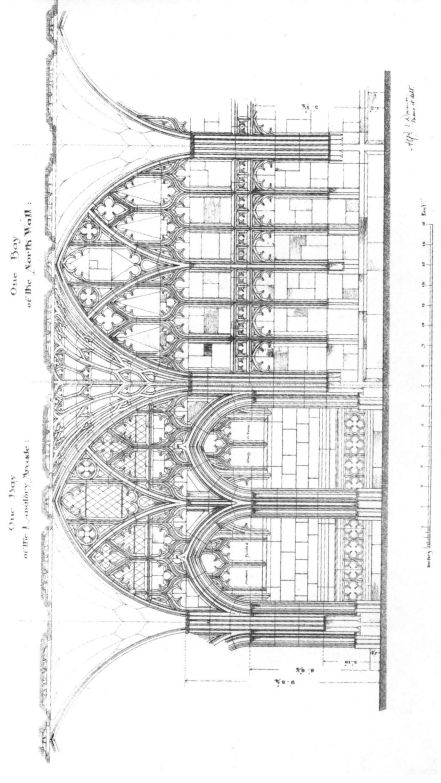

One Bay
of the North Wall:

One Bay
of the Lavatory Arcade:

Plate LII. Longitudinal Section of North Walk and Lavatory.

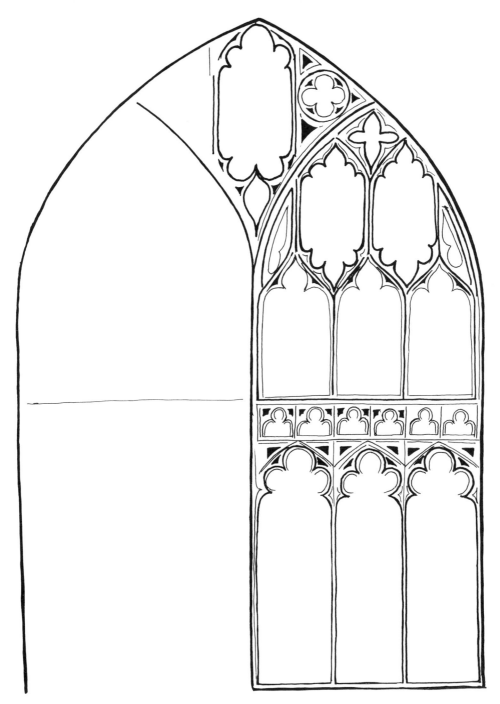

Plate LIII. Drawing of the South walk.

Plate LIV. The South walk showing the carrels on the left.

divided in each case by two main pointed arches with a horizontal element at springing level, contrived by interlacing ogee archlets. This produces two pairs of elongated hexagons above, cusped equally top and bottom, and a third pair centrally at the top, all with supermullions and Y tracery. The later work is slightly less pretty, and simpler, as the ogees do not interlace. The east walk was used as a passage communicating with other parts of the monastery. The side to the garth is divided into ten bays, nine containing a large Perpendicular window of eight lights crossed by a broad transom projecting externally like a shelf as protection from the weather. The side to the wall has corresponding blank panelling.

The other walks, as we have said, were vaulted between 1381 and 1412 and are almost but not quite indentical. There are minor changes between the east and the other sides in the tracery as well as the fans, but the whole is yet of unmatched harmony and conveys a sense of enclosure such as no other Gothic cloister. The **North Walk** contains the fan-vaulted *Lavatorium* at its west end, lit by eight two-light windows towards the garth and by a similar window at each end. Half the width is taken up by a stone ledge and trough, which originally carried a lead tank from which the water came out of spigots where the monks could wash. There was an excellent drainage system, which survives in the garth. Opposite on the north wall of the cloister, is a groined recess or almery where the towels were hung. Against the north wall a stone bench on which traces of scratchings survive indicating that the novices here played games called 'Nine Men's Morris' and 'Fox and Geese'. The west walk closely resembles the east walk, and, like it, was a mere passage, but it has a stone bench along the wall. At its southern end is the Processional Door into the nave. The **South Walk** was probably shut off by screens. It has ten windows towards the garth, but below the transom the lights are replaced by twenty little recesses or carrels. Each carrel, used for study, is lighted by a small two-light window and is surmounted within by a rich embattled cornice.

In the east walk next to the Cathedral is a door which used to give access to a wide vaulted passage leading to the monks' cemetery. This passage or **Slype** is chiefly of Early Norman date and was originally the same length as the width of the north transept against which it is built. It was entered from the cloister by a wide arch, later covered with

Plate LV. Cloisters from the south-east, engraved by Bonnor, 1796.

Plate LVI. The Chapter House when used as a Library, engraved by Bonnor, 1796.

Plate LVII. The Norman Slype or passage with its fine wall arcade, now used as the Treasury.

Perpendicular panelling. The doorway is c.1870. There is a fine Norman wall arcade on each side, with fifteen arches on the north, but only eleven on the south, the space between the flat transept buttresses admitting no more than that number. It is now the **Treasury** in which plate is exhibited, and is entered from the North transept. The roof is a plain tunnel-vault without transverse arches. The capitals are of two scallops.

In the 14th century, when the vestry and library over this passage were enlarged, the passage had to be extended to double its length. The original library stair was approached from this passage, but after the 14th century a new stair from the cloister was made, intruding into the south west corner of the Chapter House. The vestry communicates with the Cathedral only through the chapel in the North transept.

The **Library** was built in the 14th century, and retains much of its original open roof, which springs from beautiful wooden corbels. There are eleven windows on the north side, each of two square-headed lights which lit the bays or studies. The large end-windows are Late Perpendicular. None of the old fittings now survive. For several hundred years the boys from King's School (founded by Henry VIII) did all their academic work here. They used the East stair, as graffiti on the walls makes clear.

The building north of the passage is the **Chapter House.** An earlier structure existed c.1080. It is said that William the Conqueror held 'deep speech' with his Witan here at Christmas in 1085, and ordered the Domesday survey to be made, which was completed in the following year. There was originally an apse, but this was replaced with a straight but canted end. The roof is a tunnel-vault in three bays, carried by pointed transverse arches and so a second edition. The east bay is lierne-vaulted. The side walls have blank Late Norman arcades, the west end a central door flanked originally by openings and surmounted by three windows. The lower part of this wall is part of Abbot Serlo's original Chapter House, reddened by the flames which destroyed the wooden cloister in 1102.

The next opening from the cloister led to the **Dorter,** or dormitory, which no longer exists except for a fragment which can still be seen on the outside of the north east corner of the Chapter House. It is a jamb of one of the windows built at the beginning of the 14th century, with a

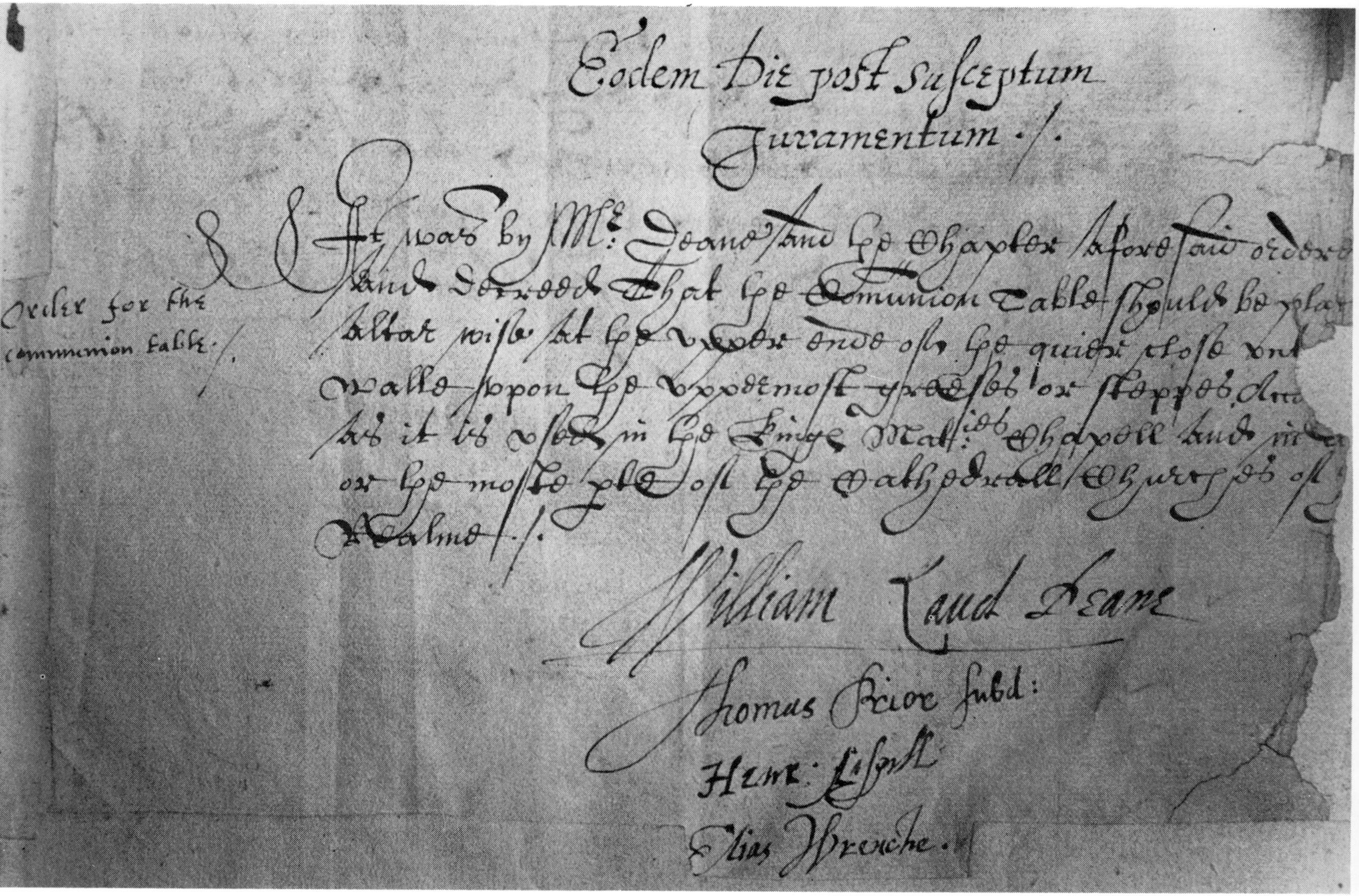

Eodem Die post susceptum
Juramentum ./

Order for the communion table ./

It was by Mr: Deane and the Chapter aforesaid ordered and decreed that the Communion Table should be placed altar wise at the upper ende of the quire close unto the walle upon the uppermost greeses or steppes, as it is used in the Kings Maties: Chappell and in [illegible] or the moste [illegible] of the Cathedrall Churches of [illegible] Realme ./

William Laud Deane

Thomas Prior subd:

Hen: [illegible]

Elias Wrenche.

Plate LVIII. The Library contains the Chapter Act Book of which the first Act is the decree of Dean Laud for the moving of the communion table to the upper end of the choir.

Plate LIX. The Library when used as College School. Engraved by Bonnor, 1796.

small ballflower decoration round the capital of a slender shaft. It was there before the Norman apse of the Chapter House was removed; for the later east end, which is square externally, has the corner cut off so as not to block the window. A Decorated string-course also runs along the Chapter House wall. The building more or less in its place, built in 1850 as an extra schoolroom for the King's School, is now used as the gymnasium.

In the north walk of the cloister there are two Early English doorways, one at each end. The eastern one opens into a 13th century vaulted passage which led to the infirmary and at a later date the Abbot's lodging. The passage is rib-vaulted in four bays with elegantly profiled arches and ribs. The **Infirmary** hall stood east to west, built like the nave of a church. There was a Chapter Order to pull it down in 1630; but in 1649 it was still standing, and its west end and six arches of the early 13th century south arcade escaped because they had been incorporated into the Babylon clutter of houses and were spared in 1860. The arcade piers have fillets, the capitals are moulded or decorated with stiff-leaf, and the arches have quite complex mouldings. It all points firmly to the 13th century.

The other door at the west end, now filled with a 19th century window, was the entrance to the refectory or frater. It has two orders of colonnettes and a richly moulded arch. This building, which was begun in 1246 on the site of the Norman one, has also disappeared, except for the lower part of the south wall, which is common to the cloister, parts of the east end and a fragment of the north wall. Under the frater was the Norman cellar; one of its responds with a fragment of the springing of the vault survives in the south east corner of the **Little Cloister,** which is built against the east end of the frater. The garth wall is Perpendicular, with five traceried openings on each side. The south side is covered by a lean-to roof, and the west walk forms part of a 15th century timber-framed house which is built over to the west of it. The north and east walks are now open, but were until quite late in the 19th century joined to a complex of chambers and houses which had evolved from the dividing up of the infirmary and lesser monastic buildings, and which was known as Babylon. **Little Cloister House,** on the west side of the Little Cloister, has 13th century remains. An Early English undercroft, probably used for storage, extends north and south beneath the

Plate LX. View of the Cloisters, Little Cloister and Little Cloister House, and the Infirmary, from the tower. In the background is the 19th century Bishops' Palace now the King's School, and in the foreground the Norman turrets of the north transept and roof of the Chapter House.

central part of the house, and there is a good external 13th century pointed-arched doorway with moulded hood facing north. Above this is the monks' **Misericord,** where they were allowed to eat meat. This building is now used by the King's School. Both it and the house next door, No. 3 Millers Green, have báck gardens on the site of the refectory. The latter house has later interest as well: the first-floor room has an early 17th century plaster ceiling decorated with a swan, a crane, and what is now the device of the Cambridge University Press inscribed 'Alma Mater Cantabrigia', so it is clear where the sacrist of those days received his education. This room also has a Jacobean overmantel and panelling. The pretty staircase with twisted balusters is early 18th century, and the ground floor rooms have typical Queen Anne panelling. The **Kitchen** stood on the north west corner of the refectory, where No. 6 Millers Green now stands.

Immediately to the north was the **Abbot's Lodging,** built in the early 14th century. It subsequently became the Bishop's Palace, was re-built in 1861 by Ewan Christian, and is now (since 1955) the King's School. The private chapel incorporated in the palace was also rebuilt by Christian and is now a library. In the 18th century it was shown to visitors by Bishop Benson, and Walpole particularly admired a stained glass window by Price. This however has not survived, though a quantity of 16th-18th century heraldic glass was put back into the Decorated-style windows of the house. Part of the wall of the original palace with Tudor windows can be seen in Pitt Street. The stabling is dated 1861 on the rain-water heads, and there is a garden house with the arms of Bishop Benson (1734-52).

Before the Abbot moved his quarters here c.1316 he lived in rooms now incorporated in **Church House** (the Old Deanery), and which during monastic times became the Prior's Lodging. It is connected with the west walk of the cloister by two doorways, but now has its main front, largely Victorian Gothic, to the west in College Green. One doorway, about the middle of the walk, opens into the court of the Prior's Lodging; the other, at the south end, opens into a vaulted passage or slype of Norman date under part of the lodging. The passage is tunnel-vaulted, and the wall shafts have scalloped capitals. The east bay looks later in its detail than the rest. The passage served as an outer parlour where the monks could talk to visitors and strangers.

Plate LXI. Church House. Two main blocks connected by the staircase turret.

It is on a lower level than the cloister, which is reached from it by a flight of steps. Over it is the Abbot's Chapel of c.1120-35, which also has a tunnel-vault and Norman wall shafts with multi-scalloped capitals. There are 15th century floor tiles at the east end. The chapel is now used as the Diocesan Secretary's Office. Both the outer parlour and the chapel have been slightly shortened and their west ends rebuilt with the old masonry in the 15th century, but the tracery of the window is 19th century. The enriched flat-arched Perpendicular external doorway into the outer parlour with its Gloucester type of cusping, though restored, is similar to the pairs of doorways in the north and south transepts leading to the ambulatory. The panelled door is dated 1614.

The buildings of Church House consist of two main blocks connected by the staircase turret. The south block, apart from containing the chapel, has three large square Norman chambers one upon the other of which plenty of visual evidence survives within. The west gable preserves the original treatment of tall, shallow panels with zigzag ornament. The two windows on the top storey have tracery comparable with the Early Perpendicular work in the south transept, but they are set under gables with arches and shafts of c.1200. Each chamber has in the north east corner a doorway for use into a garderobe which existed in 1807, when John Carter made his plan of the Cathedral. The ground-floor doorway is larger than the others and has in the arch flat foliage panels and a pellet moulding. The two lower chambers have their south east corners crossed by segmental stone arches. The lower one is moulded, the upper has chevron. They must have carried something specially heavy.

The ground floor is entered through a vaulted lobby with shafts of c.1200 with stiff-leaf and trumpet-scallop capitals. The main staircase was altered when the house was restored by Fulljames and Waller between 1863 and 1870 for Dean Law; but there are signs of 13th century work, and a medieval stone lantern on the upper flight. The most beautiful room in the north block is the **Laud Room** on the first floor, which was once part of a hall. The springing arches near the ceiling of this room reveal the original wooden structure of the roof, which may belong to the *camera hospicii* of Abbot Horton, who ruled in 1361-77. The panelling, which may not be *in situ*, was probably made

Plate LXII. The Laud Room in Church House.

late in the 16th century, before Archbishop Laud was Dean (1616-21), in a similar manner to Red Lodge at Bristol and by the same joiner; each panel contains a round-headed arched recess supported on miniature fluted pilasters and with enriched spandrels. The doorcases have fluted Ionic pilasters carrying an entablature, and the doors have the same motifs as the panels, on a larger scale, and surmounted in the top panel by a fluted fan.

The next room, known as the **Henry Room** because traditionally Henry VIII and Anne Boleyn once used it, in 1535, has an exposed timber roof with a curious type of painted decoration and a stone Tudor fireplace. To the north of this and set at right angles to it was once a much longer building, extending farther to the west than it does now, and of 13th century date. It is thought that this may have been the Abbot's Hall. Some time before the end of the 15th century it was cut down and an upper storey of wood built up on it, forming a long gallery of which the east end still remains and is called the **Parliament Room,** because it is thought that Richard II held his Parliament in the original building in 1378. The room, of exposed late 15th century half-timber construction, has been restored in 1959 by Waller & Ashwell. It contains a late 15th century wall painting removed from the monks' misericord, in Little Cloister House, and a late 14th century chimney-piece once used as a mason's setting-out table.

College Green in monastic times was divided into an outer court, which lay at the west end of the Abbey church, a lay cemetery to the south, and a monks' cemetery and garden either side of the east end with what seems to be a communicating tunnel under the Lady Chapel. It has long been thought that the precincts, which were surrounded by a wall, did not go beyond the east end of the Lady Chapel but this is by no means certain. The **Great Gate,** or St. Mary's Gate, survives at the north west corner of the outer court, leading into St. Mary's Square. It was about in the middle of the west wall of the precinct, a large part of which also still survives. On the outside it has 13th century arcading over a 13th century arched entrance with 18th century wrought-iron gates with gilded cherubs brought from Nuremberg, via Painswick church, in the early 20th century. The gateway, of three bays (two and one) of ribbed Transitional Norman vaulting, decorated with undercut chevrons, was restored by Waller.

Plate LXIII. The Great Gate or St. Mary's Gate.

Next to it was the Almoner's Lodging, and there are signs of a window for distributing food. Above it is a 16th century half-timbered house, restored by Waller and Ashwell.

The Inner Gate leading from the outer court into the inner court, now Miller's Green, has a lierne-vault. There were also two gates on the south side. King Edward's Gate is now represented only by one turret, and part of another with a stone newel stair inside, attached to which are later rooms. The rest of it was taken down when College Street was widened c.1890, and the end house of the Georgian terrace on the south side of College Green was demolished at the same time. The other gate, sometimes called St. Michael's Gate, at College Court, now consists of the remains of a small Late Perpendicular arch surmounted by a modern brick-built room.

The houses in College Green, which form a Cathedral close, were mostly rebuilt in the 18th century having been adapted from monastic to domestic use in the 16th century.

It is clear from this description of the surrounding buildings that the Cathedral was originally the church of a Benedictine Abbey. It became a Cathedral in 1541 when, following the Dissolution of the monasteries, Henry VIII formed the new diocese of Gloucester out of the diocese of Worcester. He designated the abbey church the Cathedral of the new diocese and ordered the destruction of certain of the monastic buildings.

It had been a Benedictine house since 1022, but it was not until the appointment of Serlo as abbot in 1072 that the monastery began to flourish. As we have seen much of the church he began to build remains encased within later work. Those monastic buildings which have survived the centuries, together with the Cathedral itself, are sufficient to give us a clear indication of the daily life and work of the monks.

The **Monastic day** revolved round the Hours or principal services held in the choir. These began at 2 a.m. The monks would leave their dormitory by the night stair and make their way along the east walk of the cloister, through the door into the north transept and past the stone lectern into the choir. After *Vigils*, the 'night watch' office and a period of meditation the monks remained in the choir for *Lauds* which was begun at first light. *Prime* followed at sunrise. They were back in the

Plate LXIV. View of St. Mary's Gate showing the medieval houses in St. Mary's Square before they were demolished c.1950.

choir by 9 a.m. for *Terce*, and the *Morrow Mass*.

The meeting in the Chapter House followed, presided over by the abbot or prior. Notices were given out about the services and the saints to be remembered; discipline was administered to any wayward brother (it was an obligation to inform on the misconduct of a brother monk); and the business of the day discussed. The chanting of a psalm for the dead ended the meeting.

The monks were assigned various duties for the rest of the morning, returning to the choir for *Nones* at mid-day, and this was following by *High Mass*. Mass was not one of the Hours, and in addition to this daily celebration for the whole community, those monks in the monastry who were priests were under obligation to offer the Mass daily for the living and the dead. It is for this reason that five chapels were built at each of the three levels of the eastern arm of the church, in addition to other side altars and chantries.

The evening service of *Vespers* was at 5 p.m. and this was followed, at dusk by *Compline*, which completed the Seven Hours and which, taken together, were the *Opus Dei*. The monastery existed for this purpose — the offering of continuous worship and praise to God, and to pray for the living and the departed. In later medieval times the daily offices had all sorts of variations depending on the season of the year, holy days, commemorations, processions and important festivals for which the monks were issued with copes. The cope chest in the south ambulatory dates from the fifteenth century. The basis of the music was Gregorian chant which the monks sang themselves. As time went on polyphony was introduced; but at first this was a strain of plain song which was imposed on the chant. The descant was sung by 'children of the cloister' who were in the monastery to be educated, and this introduced the treble, so gradually polyphony came into its own.

At their profession the monks took vows of lifelong poverty, chastity and obedience to the Abbot and the Rule. They were committed to staying in the monastery for the rest of their lives. This does not mean they never went outside its gates. The various officials of the house had to travel sometimes to visit dependent Houses or the estates which were the source of much of the Abbey's wealth. At other times they were called away on Court business or councils of the Church. With the founding of colleges at Oxford and Cambridge in the 14th

Plate LXV. Drawing of tiles from the presbytery.

century monks were sent to study under some renowned scholar.

In the monastery there was a daily routine of work. Some monks would work in the vineyard or herb garden, or in the field in the early days of the Abbey before servants were employed for such work. Others spent long hours studying and transcribing books in the carrels in the cloisters or in the library. Others would be engaged in teaching the 'children of the cloister' to read and write in Latin, and in training the novices of the House. Still others would be caring for the sick in the infirmary, or giving out food to the poor at the gate-house.

As the monastery increased in size and wealth the number of officials or obedientiaries increased. The chief of these under the abbot was the prior who might have one or more sub-priors responsible to him. The sacristan looked after the church and provided for its services, ensuring it was clean and tidy. The precentor had charge of the liturgical books, gospels, psalters, mass-books and choir-books, and also the library books unless there was another monk assigned to this task. The chief duty of the precentor was to lead the chant at services from the south side of the choir. The novice-master looked after the novices, instructing them in the Rule and preparing them for the demands of a monk's life.

There were other obedientiaries whose duties concerned the more mundane side of monastic life. The cellarer was often in charge of the properties of the Abbey, and also supervised the kitchen, bakery and the brewery. The cellarer's office was probably close to the store-rooms, cellars and kitchens on the north side of the cloister where the vaulted passage leading into these areas still survives. He had to see to the purchase of food, drink, clothing, and fuel, and supervise its delivery. The lay brethren, servants and tenants came under his authority. The kitchener was responsible for ensuring the meals were provided on time in the refectory and the misericord. The hosteller looked after the guests of the monastery; and the infirmarian cared for the sick. The almoner gave money, clothing, food and drink to the poor, to lepers and beggers, and visited the poor confined to their beds.

For the rest their life was communal and centred round the cloister walks. There was a general rule of silence in the cloisters, but monks could go into the western slype to talk with visitors, or the eastern slype

Plate LXVI. Watercolour by Helena Morris c.1900 showing Little Cloister House, with buttress of Infirmary on right.

to talk to one another. This was known as the locutorium. The passage led out at the eastern end to the monks' cemetery, but access to it from the east walk of the cloister is now blocked off.

The monks had opportunity of developing special skills such as illuminating manuscripts, carving in ivory, wood and stone, painting on panel and walls, working in bronze and silver, bell-founding and organ building. All these crafts were taken over by lay masters, but individual monks continued to take an active interest in them. Other monks studied medicine, and practiced it in caring for the sick in the infirmary. Others developed an interest in astronomy, geometry, architectural design, music and musical instruments, both composing and playing. The establishing of universities increased their intellectual interests and greatly enriched the life of the monasteries. Monks not only produced the books needed for worship in the scriptorium, but wrote on a variety of unusual subjects.

Far from being cut off from the life of the world the monasteries were very aware of what was going on. Gloucester was situated on important trade routes from the north, and at the Cross the road from the east led on to the more barbarous Wales. It was a market town where many gathered every week to buy and sell their wares. The monastery of St. Peter was visited by kings and queens, knights returning from the Crusades, eminent churchmen and wealthy merchants. It was often the place of retirement for elderly laymen, who spent their last days here.

The ups and downs of the monastery's economy very much depended on the administrative ability of the abbot. Abbot Staunton was such a good manager he left a thousand marks for his successor. The income was derived from estates and manors which had to be properly managed to provide what was required, particularly in view of the fact that the monks often had to pay heavy taxes both to King and Pope. Every time there was a new abbot, his appointment had to be sanctioned by the King, and the King's visits were the cause of enormous expense. Such hospitality forced from the abbot would not always have been welcome. The abbot himself, from Froucester's time 'mitred', was involved in affairs of state and therefore often away. On his return he would no doubt have had much to investigate.

Plate LXVII. The Cross in the centre of Gloucester. A medieval monument demolished in the 18th century.

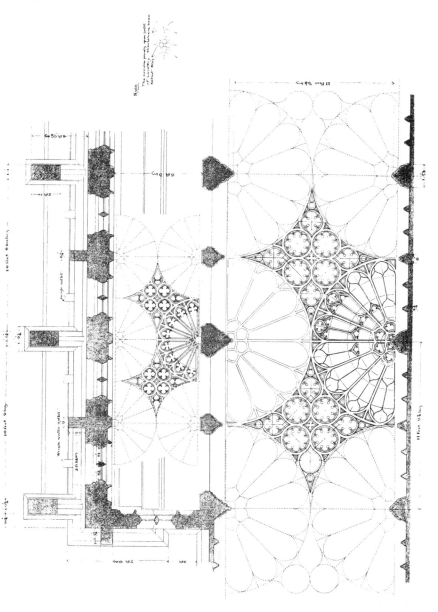

The Cloisters: Gloucester Cathedral: Nº 2.

Plan Shewing Groining to Cloisters and Lavatory North Walk.

Scale of Feet

Plate LXVIII. Plan showing groining to cloister and lavatory.

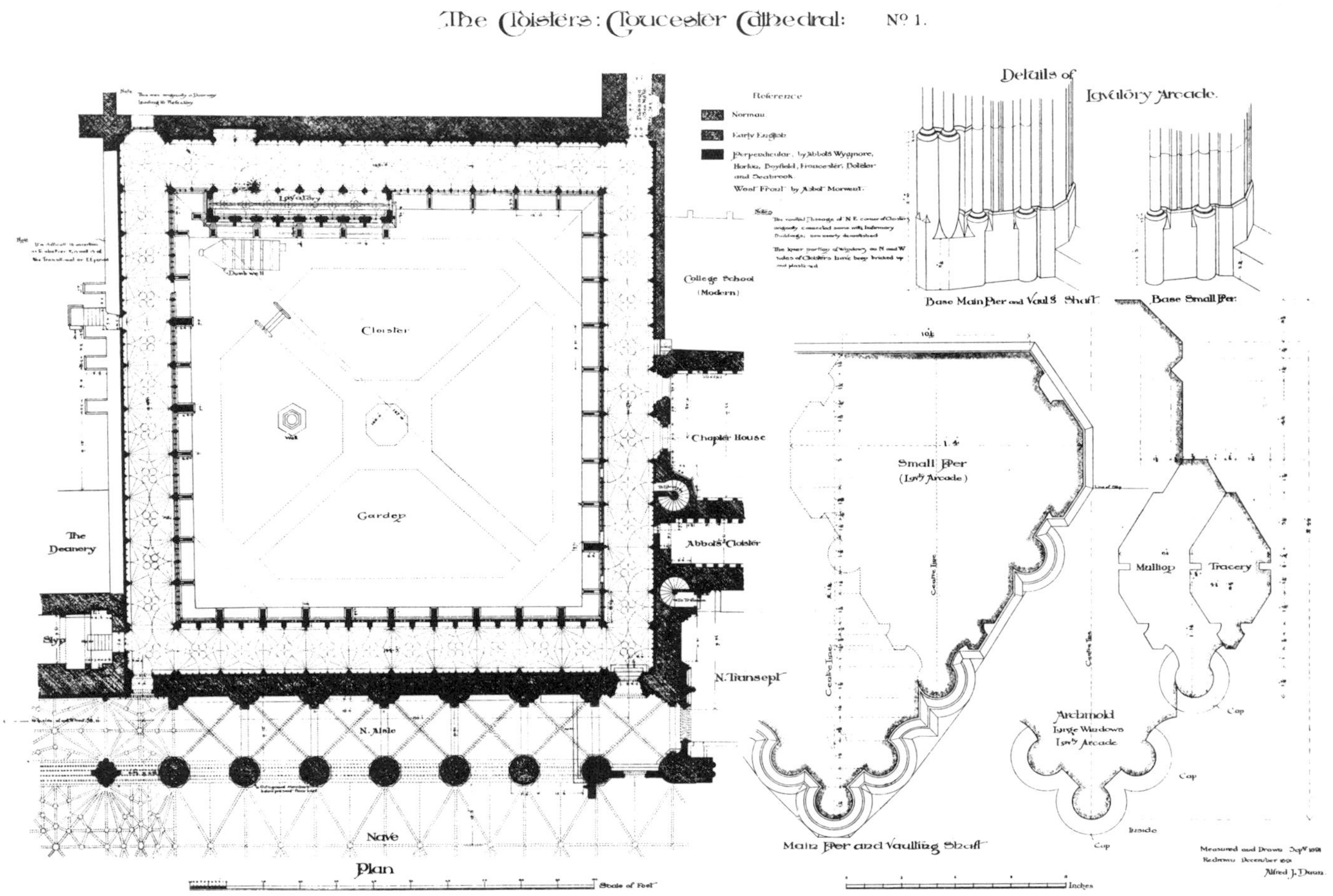
The Cloisters: Gloucester Cathedral: No. 1.
Details of Lavatory Arcade.
Reference
Norman
Early English
Perpendicular, by Abbots Wygmore, Horton, Boyfield, Frocester, Troteler and Seabrook.
West Front by Abbot Morwent.
Lavatory
Dumb well
Cloister
Garden
Well
College School (Modern)
Chapter House
Abbots Cloister
N. Transept
The Deanery
Slyp
N. Aisle
Nave
Plan
Scale of Feet
Base Main Pier and Vault Shaft
Base Small Pier
Small Pier (Lavy Arcade)
Centre line
Mullion
Tracery
Archmold Large Windows Lavy Arcade
Cap
Inside
Main Pier and Vaulting Shaft
Inches
Measured and Drawn Sept 1891
Redrawn December 1891
Alfred J. Dunn.

Plate LXIX. Plan of the Cloisters.

Plate LXX. The Great East Window.

Chapter 5

MEDIEVAL AND MODERN GLASS

Great East Window. The 14th century glazier, with few exceptions, used only white, blue, yellow, and red glass. The white glass is full of bubbles, giving that silvery light which is so apparent in this window. The blue was pure pot-metal, so that it is blue throughout. The ruby glass would have been nearly opaque if it had been red all through; so a different process was invented to produce flashed ruby glass. A yellow stain was also used which was lighter than the pot-metal and varied in many shades. For line-shading a brown enamel, made from iron, was used, or copper, if a greenish-black was required.

It is not so much the development of technique, however, which is remarkable in this window, as the development of design. The great Perpendicular window determined the design of the glass. It is the first as well as the grandest example of the window filled with tiers of full-length figures which became characteristic of the following century. The drawing of the cartoons seems closely connected with contemporary French manuscripts; the face's lack of a bottom eyelid is characteristic. The canopies, flat-fronted, are often surmounted with lofty spires; the side piers from which the arch springs run up either side into pinnacles. The background behind the figures is quite flat and richly coloured, with no attempt to produce by shading the effect of its being a hollow niche.

In this window the largest possible area for glass has been obtained by the structural necessity of deflecting outwards the side walls of the easternmost bays of the choir and by making the window a 'bow', so that it almost suggests a triptych. The subject of the window is the Coronation of the Virgin, who is attended by the apostles and saints as

Plate LXXI. The Virgin Mary in the Great East Window.

well as by the founders and representatives of the Abbey. The subject and its treatment are somewhat the same as Orcagna's contemporary triptych in the National Gallery. Above the central group of Christ and Mary (the best and least damaged figure left) enthroned are three pairs of angels holding palms. The second from the left has been lost and replaced by a 15th century Madonna from some other window. The figures on the same level as the central group represent the Twelve Apostles. The four outermost apostles on the south side have disappeared, with the exception of the feet of the last two, and have been replaced by four kings. The lower half of one of the apostles seems to have been used to replace the lower part of Christ; another may be found in the patched-up figure in the last light but one of the tier below. His large purple hat suggests St. James the Greater, who was beginning to be represented as a pilgrim in the 14th century, with a small picture of the face of Christ set in front of the hat. The much damaged figure, two to the left of this, may also be an apostle. The others in this row are canonised saints, in pairs, turning towards each other; in the left half, including the central pair, four virgin martyrs alternate with four male martyrs: St. Cecilia and St. George, a virgin whose emblem is lost and St. Edmund, St. Margaret of Antioch and St. Lawrence, St. Catherine without her wheel and St. John the Baptist. On the right there is too much confusion for certain identification.

The lower tier has figures without haloes. The place of honour in the centre is occupied by two kings, but the one on the right has been replaced by St. Edmund, who is an intruder, as the scale of the figure shows; so is the one to the right of him. The other king (left centre) may well be Edward II holding sceptre and orb, just like his recumbent effigy close by. His reputation as a quasi-saint was at its highest about this time. The inserted figures of the kings, on a larger scale but contemporary in style, may well have come from the clerestory windows. The quarries, a very large number of which survive, are ornamented with a star design or decorative insertions. The three principal tracery heads had gold flaming stars, though the central one has been replaced by a 15th century figure of St. Clement as pope. The four corresponding openings of the two wings are relieved by ornamental roundels.

The quarry lights under the lowest tier of figures are varied by a

Plate LXXII. Pair of Saints; female and knightly, in the Great East Window.

series of roundels and heraldic shields which provide the chief evidence for dating the window shortly before 1357. The four shields on the left and the four on the right occupy their original positions, and their shape is the heater-shield of the 14th century. From the left the arms are as follows: (1) Arundel, a beautiful example of streaky ruby and of a lion drawn with a lead outline. Arundel fought at the Battle of Crecy. (2) Berkeley. The greenish chevron is much later glass. (3) Warwick. Exquisite diapering of the ruby field and the yellow fesse. Warwick fought at Crecy. (4) de Bohun, also at Crecy. On the right (1) Pembroke, an early instance of the deplorable quartering. (2) Talbot, fought at Crecy. (3) Sir Maurice Berkeley, fought at Crecy, killed at Calais in 1347. (4) Thomas Lord Bradeston; note the single rose of the 14th century. He fought at Crecy and is supposed to have given this window as a memorial to Sir Maurice Berkeley. The shields in the middle are (1) Ruyhale. (2) Edward I, but earlier than the rest. (3) Edward III, showing France quarterly, repaired in 1814. (4) The Black Prince, one of the original series. (5) Henry of Lancaster. (6) Instruments of the Passion; late 15th century. Below are (1) England; late 14th century. (2) Edmund Duke of York; late 14th century. (3) Edward III; late 14th century. (4) England, Henry of Lancaster, one of the original series.

This magnificent window was probably finished by 1357. It was taken down and re-leaded by Ward & Hughes c.1862, under the superintendence of Charles Winston. No modern glass was added. The stonework was repaired in 1914. In 1939 it was again taken down and stored for safe keeping during the war years. It has recently (1976-1977) been repaired by Edward Payne of Box, near Stroud.

Lady Chapel East Window. The glass is now in such a confused and disordered state that one is hardly able to distinguish any definite subjects and carries away an impression of a mass of richly toned fragments, with here and there a face or a form dimly visible. The window generally contains work of the 14th and 15th centuries, and was reduced to this state early in the 19th century, when alien glass was also introduced. The chapel was built between 1450 and 1499, and one would therefore expect the glass to be late 15th century.

As a rule, in cases of wholesale destruction, it is in the tracery openings and the cusped heads of lights that original glass has escaped and remains in situ, and that is so here. While the three central lights at

Plate LXXIII. Heraldry in the Great East Window; bottom left 'the golfer'.

the top of the window have been filled for the most part with imported glass, some at least of the contents of the smaller side lights immediately on both sides appear to be in situ. Both represent scenes in the open air, the blue sky or landscapes being continued into the cusped heads without any canopy or framework, a pictorial method characteristic of the late 15th century. The principal figure in the one on the left is a crowned Madonna, and as there are remains of a similar figure in the small lights at both ends of the top tier, these four lights appear to be original, and illustrate miraculous stories about the Virgin.

The nine main lights of the window, divided by two transoms into three tiers, again in the cusped heads, retain much original glass similar in character to that in the tracery lights. It seems likely that unframed scenes alternated with canopied figures, as in the East window of St. Margaret, Westminster (before 1519); a compromise between the old and the new style. In the extreme right hand light of the middle of the three tiers there are the substantial remains of a Madonna in a deep red mantle with jewelled border, standing on the crescent moon in the midst of a glory of gold rays. Her head has disappeared and the Child she carried has been replaced by a mass of alien fragments. At the bottom is an inscribed band of text reading 'S(an)c(t)a Ma(ria) cel(es)t(i) lumine'. This figure must have occupied a central light.

In the eighteen round openings set between the lower transom and the heads of the lights in the bottom tier, a comb alternates with a barrel or tun, preceded on the left by an initial E and followed in the case of the comb by the syllable 'to' and in that of the tun by 'co'. Here is the rebus for Edmund Compton, the donor, who died in 1493. He was the father of Sir William Compton, a ward of Henry VII and friend of Henry VIII, and also Constable of Gloucester Castle in 1512 and of Sudeley in 1513, and Chief Steward of the Abbeys of Gloucester and Cirencester. With these Court connexions of the Comptons it is quite possible that this window was London work. This would account for the advanced form of some of the fragments both pictorial and realistic, with their considerable infusion of foreign character, particularly in the physiognomy of the full faces and the deep, rich colours of the draperies.

The three central lights at the top of the window, however, are not

Plate LXXIV. Figure of a king from the East Window of the Lady Chapel, engraved by
Samuel Lysons in 1792.

later than the middle of the 15th century and are obviously an insertion from another window. They are characteristic English work and similar to the original glass left in the windows of the north aisle of the nave. Bits of glass from side windows in the chapel, depicting the Passion, are also included, particularly the fairly well preserved Precious Blood in the central light of the middle tier, which is said to be by Richard Twygge, who worked at Malvern and at Westminster Abbey, 1507-10. Either side of this are soldier saints of the late 15th century. The bottom row of lights is mainly filled with 14th century glass, from a Jesse Tree window, probably taken from the north transept. The kings, however, must date from nearer the middle of the 14th century, and they resemble the figures in the great East window of the choir, though they do not belong to it; but the bearded face of an apostle in light one from the bottom right probably does.

There are also fragments of medieval glass in the windows of the Chantry Chapels, and at the head of the two east windows in the south transept.

In the nave there are fragments of medieval glass in the triforium windows on the north side, and also in the north aisle windows. The rest is Victorian and of varying merit.

The Great West Window. This fine window dates from the reconstruction of the west end of the Abbey Church during the abbacy of John Morwent (1421-37). It is of nine lights and in the Perpendicular style of the period. Its design resembles, particularly at the head, the Great East Window. We have no idea of the subject of the original glass, nor whether any of it is preserved elsewhere in the Cathedral. The present glass is the work of W. Wailes of Newcastle. Judged by comparison with the work of the previous century this early Victorian glazier carried out his work in pot-metal and with due regard to leading. Clearly this modern glass does not compare in colour or texture with the early medieval glass at the other end of the building, nevertheless this is a fine example of the work of the period c.1859. The window is a memorial to Bishop James Henry Monk, Bishop of Gloucester 1830-56, and was given by the Reverend T. Murray Browne, an Honorary Canon of Gloucester. The window depicts various biblical events which are illustrative of Baptism, with the

Plate LXXV. The Great West Window by William Wailes of Newcastle, in memory of Bishops Monk.

central lights depicting our Lord's Birth and the visit of the shepherds and the Magi. This theme of birth and baptism is, of course, appropriate at the west end of the Church where the font is usually placed, near the door.

In the head of the window are six crowns, and below fourteen angels, eight playing musical instruments. These angels remind us of the cluster of angels, each playing a different musical instrument, in the lierne vaulting above the high altar in the choir.

Below on four tiers are a number of scenes each occupying three lights. On the first, from the top, from left to right, is depicted the Baptism of St. Paul, the Baptism of Cornelius and the Baptism of the Jailor at Philippi recounted in the Acts of the Apostles. On the second tier there is pictured the Presentation of the infant Jesus in the Temple, with Simeon and Anna; the Baptism of Jesus; and John the Baptist preaching by the River Jordan. The third tier depicts the Nativity scenes; the angels appearing to the shepherds; the infant Jesus lying in the manger at Bethlehem; and the visit of the Magi, or Wise Men. On the bottom tier are three pictures from the Old Testament which have a symbolic significance in relation to Christian Baptism. First on the left Noah is coming out of the ark (notice the mouse just above the shell in the bottom left-hand corner); the Israelites passing through the Red Sea, with the pyramids in the background; and Naaman washing in the Jordan.

South Aisle. The large window in the west end of this aisle, and the first in the south wall are also both part of the reconstruction of the west end by Abbot Morwent in c. 1430. The other seven windows, east of the door from the south porch, were inserted during the rebuilding of the aisle by Abbot Thokey c. 1318; but the glass is 19th century.

West window is by Clayton & Bell, a firm well-known for the high standard of its work during the Victorian period. James Richard Clayton (1827-1913) and Alfred Bell (1832-95) were employed by the Dean and Chapter for work on a number of windows. This window, like so many of the period, is far too crowded. The theme is Christ's miracles of healing and raising from the dead, and we are given no less than fifteen examples, five on each of the three tiers. The window was erected in 1863 as a memorial to Dr Jenner, the discoverer of vaccination (whose statue stands close by) and his friend and biographer, Dr

John Baron.

South side (from west to east). The first window is by Hardman 1864. John Hardman & Co produced some good work of which we have several examples in the Cathedral. The colour has not the quality of medieval glass but it was an immense improvement on the enamel technique of the 18th century. The theme of this window is appropriately Justice, since it was given in memory of John Elliott, a Gloucester solicitor who died in 1864. Various Scriptural events of a legal character are depicted on two tiers, and in the head of the window are four cherubim, between two hands in glory, scales, sword, scourges and crown. On the top tier Susanna, the two elders led away to execution, after their cross-examination by the youthful Daniel. Next Moses receiving the Commandments; and on the right Ezra, the scribe, reading the law and the people weeping. On the scroll '*Ut custodiant viam, Domini et faciant indicium*'. On the lower tier there is the Judgment of Solomon; Justice with sword and scales; St. Paul before Felix, answering the accusation of Tertullus.

The second window, from the west end, like the next five are of the Decorated period. They are of three lights, and there are five sections in the head. These may be numbered from the topmost section (1) then left (2) and right (3) and then below on the left (4) and to the right (5). The glass is by Bell of Bristol 1861, and as the inscription indicates it is a memorial to Maria Evans of Minsterworth d.1848. It depicts certain Beatitudes and Christian virtues, and works of mercy, so that in the head of the window we have (1) Blessed are the poor in spirit (2) Faith (3) Hope (notice the anchor) (4) Blessed are those who mourn (5) Blessed are the meek (Christ washing the disciples' feet). On the first tier the three scenes show the relieving of the hungry; Christ telling the disciples 'In as much . . . ', and visiting the sick. On the second tier we have giving drink to the thirsty; taking in and clothing the stranger, and visiting those in prison.

The third window is by Warrington of London 1856. It is not a good example of his work. It is confused both in theme and design. Like other windows in this aisle it suggests the donors of the windows had far too great an influence in their design, and the Dean and Chapter exercised too little control. This window is a memorial to General Sir W.G. Davy, and was given by members of his family. In the head is

Christ, surrounded by four angels. In the centre of the window we have Ecce Homo (St. John 19.5), on the left the Annunciation and on the right Mary Magdalene meeting the risen Christ in the Garden. Above are three angels holding shields containing from the left a ladder and three nails, IHS in a crown of thorns, and a cross and spear, sponge and hyssop. Below are three angels with Peter's sword and Malchus' ear; the arms of the Davy family, and the third angel with scourge and whipping pillar. Note the background of scroll work.

The fourth window is by Clayton and Bell, given by 'many friend's in memory of Sir. W. Guise Bt. + 1834. It depicts the Coronation at Gloucester in 1216 of Henry III, aged nine, with a circlet of gold, the regalia having been lost in Lincolnshire by King John. In the head are the armorial bearings of (1) Sir William Guise (2) De Burgh (3) Beauchamp (4) Guise and Wright (5) Guise and Vernon. In the centre we have Henry III crowned by Gualo (the Papal legate) and Peter des Roches, Bishop of Winchester. Below, *Henricus rex in ecclesia Gloucestrie coronatus.* On the left is Hubert de Burgh, Earl of Kent, standing with sword drawn, three nobles in mail and a Bishop or Abbot. On the right is Joceline, Bishop of Bath, standing with four nobles in mail. Below in two tiers are the armorial bearings of De Burgh, Beauchamp, Mauditt, De Bellomonte, Kenne and Snell; and on the lower tier Wysham, D'Abitot, Newburgh, Fitzwith, Cooke and Guise.

The fifth window is by Bell of Bristol 1860. It is in memoriam Mary Evans, d.1837. The theme is the *True Vine.* In the head is depicted the widow offering her mite, and below left and right St. Matthew and St. Mark seated. Below them is Jesus, Martha and Mary on the left and Mary Magdalene washing Jesus's feet. On the first tier Christ is foretelling the destruction of Jerusalem; centre, Christ between six angels, and on the right Christ pointing to the lilies of the field. On the lower tier, the Good Samaritan, above St. Luke is seated; Christ telling Peter to feed His sheep, and on the right the Return of the Prodigal, with St. John seated above. The background of trailing vine is rather overdone; indeed the whole window is rather gaudy.

The sixth window is by Clayton and Bell, 1859, and depicts the most historical occasion associated with the Cathedral, the funeral of Edward II, 1327. In the head of the window we see the King being led

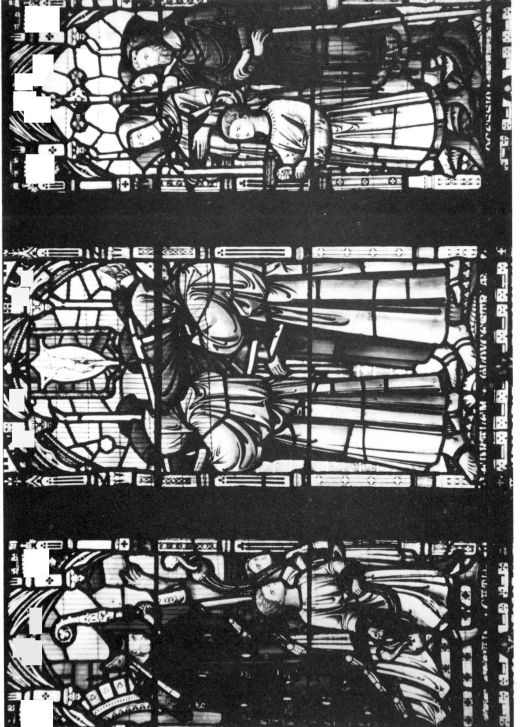

Plate LXXVI. Window by Clayton & Bell, 1859, depicting the burial of Edward II.

prisoner to Berkeley Castle, and below to the left and right the arms of the Abbey (without the sword) and of the King respectively. Then below the Murder of the King, and the Abbot receiving the King's body and placing a pall on it. The three central lights form one scene, a procession of monks and others bring the King's body to the Abbey, and at the door it is received by Abbot Thokey. In the lower tier is depicted the Burial of the King on the north side of the presbytery, the erection of the tomb, and peasants offering flowers at his shrine.

The seventh window by Warrington 1858, is a memorial to Jeremiah Balme + 1857. In the head of the window is the Holy Lamb with a banner with medallions below on either side, and below them angels with censers. In the centre Christ on the Cross, with Mary and John standing by; on the canopy is an angel holding armorial bearings and the motto *Fortiter et Recte*. On the left is depicted the giving of the talents by the King (St. Matt. 25.14) and on the right the returning of the talents. On the side canopies are two angels with scrolls proclaiming 'The memory of the — just is blessed'.

The eighth window. Up the steps, and above the Bridges' tomb is a larger window than the others in this aisle, and quite different in design. The glass is by Rogers of Worcester 1855. It is of four lights, in the upper tier are the four Evangelists, and in the lower St. Stephen, two Christian knights and St. Peter. The inscription gives details of its dedication and the donor.

North Aisle. The window of four lights at the west end of the aisle is by Hardman, and is a memorial to W. Viner Ellis of Minsterworth 1865. It depicts scenes from the legendary British King, Lucius, who according to tradition was buried in Gloucester. In the head are four crowned figures in armour, left to right, Robert, Duke of Normandy 1134, Thomas of Woodstock 1397, Humphrey 1447 and William Frederick 1834, all three Dukes of Gloucester. In the lower tier we see Lucius being crowned by the Druids, and Lucius sending a messenger to Rome to request the Pope to baptise him. In the upper tier Lucius is baptised, and on the right his funeral procession.

Above the entrance to the cloisters is a window of four lights only half open. It depicts the burial and resurrection of Jesus (Clayton and Bell).

The second window and the next six are of three lights set within the original Norman openings. This window contains glass by Ward and Hughes 1860, and depicts, as female figures, Faith with cross and chalice, Charity with children and Hope with an anchor.

The third window contains old glass restored by Hardman, the lower part however is chiefly new glass. In the head St. John the Baptist, and St. Margaret holding a cross-headed spear transfixing a dragon. On either side an angel with censer. Below, left to right, St. Patrick as bishop, St. Oswald as king and St. James the Great.

The fourth window is by Clayton and Bell 1858, and is a memorial to Dr G.W. Hall, Master of Pembroke College, Oxford and Prebendary of the Cathedral. The window depicts various events connected with the birth of Christ.

The fifth window contains old glass restored by Hardman. In the head we see St. Thomas of Canterbury and St. Catherine with wheel and sword. And below, left to right, St. Dorothy with a basket of flowers, St. George spearing the Dragon and St. Thomas as bishop.

The sixth window, by Clayton and Bell, is to Bishop Hooper who was burned to death in St. Mary's Square February 9th 1555. It depicts the martyrdoms of St. John, Bishop Hooper and St. Laurence. It was given by Charlotte Claxson c. 1860.

The seventh window also by Clayton and Bell 1860, is a memorial, as the inscription states, to Thomas Turner a benefactor of the poor and sick. In the head are armorial bearings and motto, and below the empty sepulchre visited by the two Maries and Joanna. The three main lights depict Christ raising Jairus' daughter, the healing of the crippled man at the Pool of Bethesda, and the raising of the widow's son at Nain. In the base are figures of twelve Apostles, including St. Paul and St. Matthias, omitting St. James the Great, with their emblems.

The eighth window is a memorial to members of the Darell family, and is by Preedy of London, 1864. The main lights depict the Risen Lord, St. John the Evangelist, and the Virgin Mary with lily and pomegranate. Like the previous window this one is larger than the others in the north aisle, but though pointed it appears to be set within the original Norman opening.

Fragments of painted glass remain in the clerestory windows. One (the third from the west end on the north side) has been restored to the original design, namely, quarries ornamented with roses, central medallions, stars in foliations and borders of crowns.

South Transept. Some of the oldest glass in the Cathedral is to be found in the upper east windows of this transept. It consists of white scroll work of vine leaves, on a ruby ground, in the heads; and plain quarries with simple borders, below. It was restored by Hardman, c.1865. The large window in the west wall is by Kempe. There are four angels in the head, two with scrolls and two with musical instruments. Below in the four main lights are named figures, with scenes beneath them on the theme of Music and the Arts.

The windows in the chapel of St. Andrew have glass by Hardman. The great south window is by Hardman; subject, life of St. Peter.

North Transept. The windows in the chapel of St. Paul on the east side of the transept contain glass by Burlison and Grylls, 1870. In the centre our Lord is seated in Majesty, surrounded by adoring angels, bearing crowns and palms. The two side lights have angels playing musical instruments reminiscent of the angelic choir over the high altar.

The Great Window is by Hardman, 1876, and was given by the family in memory of Sir Michael Hicks-Beach, Bart., M.P. It depicts scenes from the life of St. Paul as told in the Acts of the Apostles.

The west window, like the one in the corresponding position in the south transept is by Kempe 1894. From the principal figures, Bezaleel, Solomon, St. Gregory and St. John Chrysostom, the theme of the window is apparently Law and Learning. The window is too full of detail and the canopy work is overdone, but nevertheless it is a fine example of Kempe's work.

South Ambulatory of the choir contains three windows by Kempe. From the west the first depicts Anselm, Archbishop of Canterbury, Elizabeth mother of St. John the Baptist, St. Christopher, and Elizabeth of Hungary 1207-1231. It is difficult to see the theme of this grouping and one suspects it is a highly individual selection by the family of Canon Richard Harvey 1889 and his wife to whom the window is dedicated. The next window, a memorial to Dean Henry Law 1884, has figures of Adam, Noah, Abraham and Moses with a scene from the story of each below.

The last window commemorates Sir John Seymour Bart for over fifty years a Canon of Gloucester, 1880. The figures are Isaiah, St.

John the Baptist, our Lord and St. John the Evangelist. Again below the figures are scenes from the life of each.

North Ambulatory also contains three windows by Kempe c. 1892. From the west they depict four abbots, four patron saints and four holy women. The four abbots are Osric, Serlo, Wigmore and Seabroke with a scene from the history of the Abbey associated with each. The four patron saints are St. Patrick, St. Michael, St. George and St. Columba; and the four holy women, Martha, Catherine, The Virgin Mary and Mary Magdalene. In the chapel at the east end of the ambulatory, the Memorial Chapel, the windows contain fragments of old glass but otherwise they are glazed with clear glass.

The clerestory windows on the north side of the presbytery contain some old glass in the heads, all restored by Clayton and Bell, otherwise the full length figures, all named, are almost entirely 19th century glass. The original glazing had figures under canopies, some of the upper portions of which have escaped destruction and are incorporated in the figures. Some of the misplaced figures in the great East Window may have been removed from the clerestory, and fragments of other figures may be in the mosaic of the east window of the Lady Chapel. On the south side the clerestory windows are in grisaille by Hardman.

Lady Chapel contains some fine glass by Christopher Whall (1850-1924) in conjunction with his son and daughter, Christopher and Veronica Whall. The figures of the saints are named. The first window from the west on the north side was given in memory of John Dearman Birchall + 1897. The second depicts the Annunciation, and opposite on the south side the Nativity. The window on the north side of the sanctuary shows Christ in Majesty. It was Christopher Whall who coined the phrase when speaking to his pupils 'Let your colours sing' and these fine window vividly illustrate the maxim. In the chapel on the north side is a window by Kempe 1895, and opposite in the south chapel are fragments of medieval glass in the heads of the south windows. The east window is described on p. 119.

Cloisters. It was decided by the Dean and Chapter in the mid-19th century to reglaze the windows of the cloisters, as donors could be found, with glass which would tell the story of our Redemption. The east walk was completed together with the lavatorium but the rest remains to be done. Apparently the plan which begins with the Fall in the Garden of Eden, and the Prophets announcing the Coming of Christ, was to tell the story of the Gospels in considerable detail.

East walk, south to north: first window by Hardman, and the following six windows all by Hardman, eighth window by Ballantine, ninth by Hardman, tenth by Clayton & Bell. The ten small two-light windows in the Lavatorium by Hardman. A few other windows by Hardman in the other walks. The best glass is in the South walk, but this is not 19th century: it is mostly 16th century glass from Prinknash Abbey, six panels having been taken to Prinknash by Abbot Parker, the last Abbot of Gloucester, and the rest by Lady Chandos of Sudeley. Woodforde writes: 'A much higher standard was maintained in the 16th century in drawing of heraldry than figures. Representations of Royal Arms and badges are particularly good'. Here are excellent examples, including the badge of Katherine of Aragon (pomegranate). Before the re-glazing of the cloisters, J. T. Niblett recorded seven examples of the Plantagenets' *planta genista* in the lavatorium windows.

Plate LXXVII. The Norman face in the crypt.

Chapter 6

EFFIGIES EVERYWHERE

Gloucester Cathedral has its fair share of effigies and memorials. Some are of considerable artistic achievement, others of historic importance, and many others, whether to the famous or to the obscure, of great human interest.

There is no Norman figure sculpture in the Cathedral, with the possible exception of a 'face' to be found on one of the capitals in the crypt. The lead font now housed in the triforium, came from a derelict church in the Wye valley. There is, however, the effigy of **Robert, Duke of Normandy** in the presbytery, which must be earlier than 1219 and is possibly as early as 1160. He is not wearing poleyns on his knees and his chain-mail suggests mid 12th century. The eldest son of William the Conqueror, he made war against his father. He went on the first Crusade in 1096 where he played quite a distinguished part; but he was greatly incensed that he was left Normandy and his younger brother William Rufus England. He had an engaging and likeable character but lacked the drive of his brother, afterwards Henry I, who captured him in 1107. He died in prison in Cardiff in 1134 and desired to be buried in Gloucester Abbey. On the effigy he is wearing a moustache. The body is protected by a hooded hauberk of mail reaching nearly to the knees over which is a sleeveless surcoat. He wears a coronet of strawberry leaves and fleur-de-lis. The effigy rests on a chest-tomb of 15th century workmanship with an iron hearse framework for supporting a pall. Along the sides are the attributive shields of the Nine Worthies, part of a late 15th century cult, and facing east that of England quartered with France. The effigy is before the High Altar though he was probably buried in the Chapter House. During World War II the effigy was put

Plate LXXVIII. Robert Courthose, Duke of Normandy.

Plate LXXIX. Abbot Serlo, the first Norman abbot: 13th century effigy.

in the crypt with the Coronation Chair from Westminster, and as Mr. Bernard Ashwell has wryly pointed out Duke Robert got nearer to the throne in the 20th century than ever he did in his lifetime.

Nearby, on the south side of the Presbytery is a 13th century stone effigy, supported on a cradle, thought to represent **Abbot Serlo,** the first Norman Abbot and founder of the Abbey church. The arch of the canopy over the head terminates in two diminutive heads. Below is a foliated boss representing maple leaves, naturalistic, not conventional. The monument cannot be earlier than c.1280. The effigy was probably moved from the north side when the original position was given over to Osric.

In the **South Ambulatory** is a Gothic tomb-chest with angels and rich canopy, with no effigy. The style is c.1300 but it is a memorial to the Reverend John Kempthorne + 1838. Further to the east and on the opposite side of the ambulatory is an imposing memorial to Bishop Ellicott + 1905. It is an alabaster tomb-chest and figure, and is by a local sculptor, W.S. Frith. The Bishop was one of the revisers of the Authorised Version at the end of the last century. A considerable Biblical scholar he wrote a number of commentaries on the Greek text of the New Testament.

Passing into the Lady Chapel immediately on the north side is a towering memorial to John Powell + 1713, signed by Thomas Green of Camberwell. It is a standing effigy of a judge, in marble, a noble figure by one of the outstanding statuaries of the first quarter of the 18th century. Nearly opposite on the wall is a bronze tablet by Drury with an inscription by Eric Gill c.1907 to Dorothea Beale, the founder and first Principal of Cheltenham Ladies' College. The tablet nearby with a frontal kneeling figure is to Margery Clent + 1623 a daughter of Bishop Miles Smith. On the north wall, opposite is a memorial to another daughter of the Bishop, Elizabeth, wife of W.J. Williams. The effigy lies on its side, with an infant on a pillow. The Latin inscription runs:

'Husband, you carved in marble here your wife
Thus you'd ensure her immortality.
But Christ my hope and trust was all my life,
So God forbids that I should mortal be.'

LXXX. Elizabeth Williams, daughter of Bishop Miles Smith; early 17th century.

Dr Miles Smith became Bishop of Gloucester in 1612. He was a classical scholar and Hebraist. He was involved in the translation of the Bible in 1607 and is supposed to have written the Preface of the Authorised Version, 1611, the literary masterpiece which has influenced the whole English way of life. Miles Smith sympathised with the Puritans and disliked ceremonial; in fact he had much in common with Bishop Hooper. It was unfortunate for him that William Laud was made Dean of Gloucester during his episcopate. Laud, before coming to Gloucester had already denounced the presbyterians at Oxford and declared his intention to reform the church. Confident of King James' support he set about his task in Gloucester with little regard for the views of the Bishop, Dr. Miles Smith. At the first meeting of the Chapter on January 25th, 1616; 'it was by the Dean and Chapter ordered that the Communion Table should be placed altar-wise at the upper end of the Choir, close to the wall on the uppermost steps according as it is used in the King's chapel'. He then placed a communion rail (part of which is now in the Lady Chapel) in front, so as to prevent dogs fouling the sanctuary — the first Laudian communion rail. He considered that Holy Communion should be received kneeling, and on entering the church people should bow to the altar, all of which became common practice in the 19th century; but Bishop Miles Smith said he would never set foot in the Cathedral again. Tempers were cooled by the efforts of Alderman John Jones who imprisoned certain militant Puritans. Jones was registrar to eight Bishops and so must have had considerable experience. His delightful monument with a painted half-length upright effigy, full of nice details like the packets of deeds dated 1581-1630, can be seen on the west wall of the nave within the Book-stall. In 1621, Laud left to become Bishop of St. Davids, after five stormy years in Gloucester. He did not bother to try to win over his opponents by persuasion, and this was the cause of his ultimate failure when after being Archbishop of Canterbury he was beheaded. Miles Smith lived till 1624, and presumably he did enter the Cathedral again. His two daughters both died in childbirth, and as we have seen, have charming monuments in the Lady Chapel. His own monument is a plain marble slab with no name, only identified by his arms impaled with those of the See.

In the north ambulatory there is a monument to **Osric,** which

Plate LXXXI. Edward II. The most thrilling of all tomb canopies.

Plate LXXVII. Edward II. Alabaster London work, c. 1330.

however only dates from c. 1530. Osric was honoured by Abbot Parker as the founder of the monastery, and his sister Kyneburg was the first Abbess, at the end of the 7th century. The effigy is rudely carved, perhaps in imitation of an earlier figure, and lies on a tomb-chest, above which is a Tudor canopy with a panelled soffit. In the spandrels on the north side the arms of Abbot Parker and the attributed arms of Northumbria.

The effigy of **Edward II** is of alabaster and London work of c. 1330. The canopy is fine-grained oolitic limestone from the Cotswolds, probably Painswick; plaster is used only for the points. Restoration of the canopy was undertaken three times in the 18th century by Oriel College, Oxford. The tomb-chest on which the effigy rests is made of Purbeck marble, with ogee-arched recesses, cinquefoiled with crocketed heads. The canopy consists of two stages of ogee-headed arches with close cusping at the sides of the arches and ogee foils — the work of a genius — surmounted by finials with buttresses placed diagonally and terminating in pinnacles. It may well be called the most thrilling of all tomb canopies. Large ogee-headed niches have been cut away from the Norman piers at either end of the shrine. The capitals were painted brown with a motif of white harts after the visit of Richard II in 1378.

The next monument is that of the last Abbot, **William Parker,** the effigy carved of alabaster c. 1535. It was prepared for him, but after the Dissolution he was not buried here; instead a Marian and an Elizabethan Bishop lie below. Parker's effigy is vested in full pontificals, including his mitre (the Abbots had been mitred since c. 1381). It lies on a high tomb with three panels on each side, the first and third bearing emblems of the Passion and the middle one the arms of Parker. In the frieze above are the Tudor rose, the pomegranate, a lion's head, oak leaves, fleur de lys, and the initials W.M. for William Malvern (alias Parker). At the head, the Norman pier has been mutilated, and the Abbot's arms are placed here surmounted by a mitre. The floor is paved with medieval tiles. The monument has close Perpendicular screens to left and right.

In the north transept, on the west side, is the large painted stone monument to **John Bower** + 1615 and Ann his wife. The figures are painted. They kneel, the males facing the females. Here too is a plaque

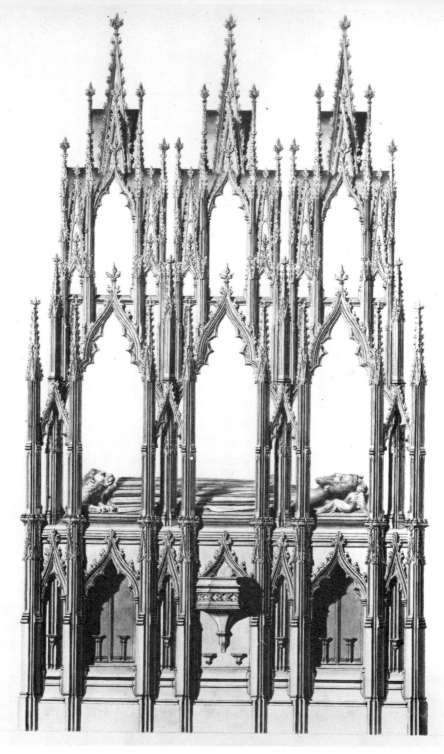

Plate LXXXIII. Edward II. Carter's drawing of the tomb.

Plate LXXXIV. Abbot William Parker, alias Malvern, c. 1535.

to the memory of a Georgian Dean of Gloucester, Dr. Josiah Tucker, 'who in the long period of 42 years during which he filled that station was never once obliged by sickness or induced by inclination to omit or abridge a single residence, and the state of the fabric at the time of his death bore ample testimony to the conscientious and liberal interest which he always took in the preservation and improvement of it'.

Across in the south transept is an impressive tomb-chest with recumbent effigies of Alderman Abraham **Blackleech** + 1639 and his wife Gertrude, according to Mrs. Esdaile by either Epiphanius Evesham or Edward Marshall. They are similar to the effigies of Sir William and Lady Sandys at Miserden. The recumbent effigies are carved in alabaster with very perfect attention to the details of the clothing. His feet rest on an eagle and hers on a mailed fist holding a dagger. They lie on a black marble tomb-chest and are good examples of the Nicholas Stone period, whoever they are by. Along side is the monument to Richard Pates + 1588 the founder of the Pates Grammar School in Cheltenham and builder of Matson House. The effigies have disappeared, but the painted stone Elizabethan canopy remains.

Other monuments in the south transept are as follows. Marble bust of T.B. Lloyd-Baker + 1886 by W.S. Frith, the bust in relief in a medallion above a relief of Justice. Small brass and marble tablet to Canon Evan Evans + 1891, by Henry Wilson. Tablet to Benjamin Baylis + 1777, by Bryan of Gloucester. Mary, wife of Thynne Gwynne + 1808, by Reeves of Bath. Canon Trotter + 1913 and Canon Scobell + 1917, nice, rich tablets of the period.

In the **South Aisle,** near the south transept, are the recumbent effigies of a **Knight and his Lady,** in a 14th century canopied tomb which has an ogee arch with foliated crockets and finial. It is panelled at the sides and back and has a vaulted roof without bosses, like the roof of the south transept. On either side is a canopied niche. The ogee arches are three-dimensional with pinnacles. The Knight is said to be Sir Thomas Brydges of Coberley and he wears the SS collar, a Lancastrian badge instituted by Henry IV; therefore the effigy must be early 15th century. The lady also has an SS collar. In the chapel opposite is the recumbent figure of **Abbot Seabroke** + 1457. On his head he wears the *mitra pretiosa*, and in his right hand he carries his pastoral staff, the head of which is missing. His stole and maniple have deep fringes; the

Plate LXXXV. Alderman Blackleech and his wife, in the manner of Nicholas Stone.

Plate LXXXVI. Early 15th century effigies of a knight and his lady wearing the SS

Plate LXXXVII. Abbot Seabroke, + 1457.

tunic and dalmatic are plain. The alb is very long almost covering his feet. The hands are missing; on his feet he wears plain pointed sandals, they rest on a lion, carved like the figure from alabaster. Also in this chapel is a memorial to Francis Baber + 1669. It is a large tablet, fixed to the Norman pier, with twisted columns and emblems of death. It has an open segmental pediment.

In the **South Aisle** are the following tablets. Mary Clarke + 1792, by W. Stephens of Worcester, and Richard Clarke + 1796, by the same sculptor. Prebendary William Adams + 1789, by T. King of Bath. Jane Webb + 1811, by Wood of Gloucester. John Webb of Norton Court + 1795, by Bryan of Gloucester in classical taste. Mary Singleton + 1761, by J. and J. Bryan. Coloured marbles, Baroque style. Sir George Onesiphorus Paul + 1820. Paul, the great prison reformer, we are told was 'a man endeared to his friends by many virtues, both public and private, but who claims this mark of local respect by having first reduced to practice the principles which have immortalised the memory of Howard. For to the object of this memorial it is to be ascribed that this county has become the example and model of the best system of criminal discipline in which provident regulation has banished the use of fetters and health has been substituted for contagion, thus happily reconciling humanity with punishment and the prevention of crime with individual reform'. The freestanding bust is by Sievier. It is set on a large marble sarcophagus. Sir John Guise of Higham + 1794, by Millard of Gloucester. A draped broken column. Dame Mary Strachan + 1770, by Ricketts of Gloucester, who has produced a monument, well above the usual provincial level; this one and the one to the Bishop of St. David's nearby are outstanding even for their date. A cherub holds Lady Strachan's portrait in a medallion, very elegant decoration, and underneath are the Baronet's arms with delightful little contemporary male supporters. Richard Raikes + 1823, by Rickman in the Gothic style. Eli Dupree + 1707. The bust is on top in a broken pediment. Gaoler Cunningham + 1836. Erected by the Magistrates, by the south door. Bishop William Nicholson + 1671. Anthony Ellys, Bishop of St. David's + 1761, by Ricketts; excellent detail. Jane Fendall + 1799, by King of Bath. Alderman John Jones, c.1630. Painted, half-length upright effigy, by Southwark workshops; a monument full of delight-

JENNER

Plate LXXXVIII. Dr. Edward Jenner, benefactor of mankind and discoverer of vaccination.

ful details such as the packets of deeds as though in pigeonholes and dated 1581-1630, for as we have said he was registrar to eight Bishops. Hubert Parry, musician + 1918. Statue of Dr. Edward Jenner, who first used vaccination, by R.W. Sievier, London 1825.

In the **North Aisle,** against the west wall are tablets to Bishop Martin Benson + 1752, and Bishop Warburton + 1779, by T. King of Bath. Along the north wall, from the west end, there is first a large monument to Charles Brandon Trye + 1811, with bust in a medallion held by two life-size angels. Three pretty medallions to three members of the famous Gloucester bell-making family of Rudhall: Abraham Rudhall + 1798, Charles Rudhall + 1815, and Sarah Rudhall + 1805. Tablet to the Rudge family by Millard. Colonel Edward Webb + 1839, by H. Hopper of London. Conventional mourning female; Gothic. Samuel Hayward of Wallsworth Hall + 1790, by Bryan of Gloucester. Ralph Bigland, Garter Principal King of Arms + 1784. Hester Gardner + 1822, by James Cooke. The last three are good classical monuments in a group together. Sarah Morley died at sea in 1784, in passage from India. It is by Flaxman, the fashionable 18th century sculptor. She embarked with 'her young family when their health and education required their removal to England, and having sustained the pains of childbirth at sea she died a few days after that event on 25th May, 1784 in the 29th year of her age'. Three angels receive her and her baby from the rolling waves. Classical in style, Gothic in feeling. Various tablets by Millard & Cooke of Gloucester. Tablet to Albert Mansbridge, 'Founder of the Workers' Educational Association. Born in this city and first educated in the Parish Elementary School of St. James', he rose by virtue of his intellectual gifts and moral strength to high eminence as a teacher, writer and benefactor to his fellow men and a great Christian, 1876-1952'. Next is a monument to Alderman Thomas Machen and his wife Christian. It is a painted monument of c.1615 (perhaps by Samuel Baldwin of Stroud). He was Mayor of Gloucester and kneels opposite his wife. Above them is a horizontal canopy supported by Corinthian columns. The monuments in the Cathedral have been re-painted at different times, for instance for the Three Choirs Festival in 1797, but Machen the Mayor has his original red gown. Beside the memorial is one to Canon E.D. Tinling + 1897. It shows a bronze figure kneeling and marble details; a fine

Plate LXXXIX. Sarah Morley, by John Flaxman.

154

example of the period of Henry Wilson. And opposite is the most recent memorial, a tablet by B. Fedden to Ivor Gurney, poet and musician of Gloucester + 1937.

Acknowledgements

We would wish to express our indebtedness to several people who have made our understanding of the building very much clearer through their printed work, correspondence, and conversation, Dr. John Harvey, author of 'The Perpendicular Style', the former Dean, the Very Rev. S.J.A. Evans, C.B.E. and Mr. Bernard Ashwell, the Cathedral Architect. We are also grateful to the present Dean, the Very Rev. Gilbert Thurlow, who has himself done so much for the Cathedral by rehanging the bells and creating the Treasury.

We also wish to thank Mr. Jack Farley who took all the photographs in the book, except Nos. VII, XI, XXVIII, LVIII, and LXXXV which were kindly taken by Mr. Peter Turner. We also thank the Society of Antiquaries of London for supplying Nos. II, IX, IXX, XX, XXV, XXXIX, XLIII, and LXXXIII, the British Library No. V, Arlington Mill Museum, Bibury, Nos. LXVI, and LXVII, and the Gloucester City Library, (Gloucestershire Collection) Nos. XIV, XV, XVI, XXI, XLVII, LV, LVI, LIX, LXVIII, LXIX, and LXXIV.

David Verey
David Welander

GLOSSARY

Note. The sign + is used for died.

AMBULATORY. Semicircular or polygonal aisle enclosing an apse. A place to walk in.

APSE. Vaulted semicircular or polygonal end of a chancel or a chapel.

BALLFLOWER. Stone carved globular flower of three petals enclosing a small ball. A decoration used in the first quarter of the 14th century particularly in the west of England.

BOWTELL. The shaft of a clustered pillar: also used for any plain round moulding, from its resemblance to the staff of an arrow or bolt.

CHANTRY. Chantry chapel attached to, or inside, a church endowed for the saying of Masses for the soul of the founder or some other individual.

CHEVRON. Norman moulding forming a zigzag.

CORBEL. A projecting stone, usually carved, to support some feature on its horizontal top surface.

CROSSING. Space at the intersection of nave, chancel and transepts.

CRYPT. Underground room usually below the east end of a church

CUSP. Projecting point between the foils in a foiled Gothic arch.

DECORATED. Historical division of English Gothic architecture covering the period between c.1290 to c.1350. Terminology invented by Thomas Rickman in the 19th century and still in use today.

EARLY ENGLISH. Historical division of English Gothic architecture roughly covering the 13th century.

FAN-VAULT. Late medieval vault where all ribs springing from one springer are of the same length, the same distance from the next, and the same curvature.

FLAMBOYANT. Probably the latest phase in French Gothic architecture where the window tracery takes on wavy undulating lines.

FOIL. Lobe formed by the cusping of a Gothic arch, or circle. Trefoil, quatrefoil, cinquefoil express the number foils, or small arcs in Gothic tracery.

FOUR-CENTRED ARCH. Late medieval form of arch consisting of four curves drawn from four different centres.

GROIN VAULT. Or Cross Vault, consisting of two tunnel vaults of identical shape intersecting each other at right angles, chiefly in Norman architecture.

LANCET. Slender pointed-arched window.

LIERNE. Tertiary rib in a vault, that is a rib which does not spring either from one of the main springers or from the central boss. Introduced in the 14th century.

MISERICORD. Bracket placed on the underside of a hinged choir stall seat which, when turned up, provided the occupant with a support during long periods of standing (also called miserere). It also means an appartment of a monastery where some indulgences were permitted such as eating meat.

MULLION. Vertical (stone) posts or uprights dividing a window into lights.

OGEE. Arch, introduced c.1300 and specially popular in the 14th century, formed by the combination of a round and hollow.

PARCLOSE. A carved timber screen or partition generally enclosing an altar or chantry chapel.

PERPENDICULAR. Historical division of English architecture covering the period from c.1335-50 till the Tudor period or c.1530.

PULPITUM. Stone screen in a major church provided to shut off the choir from the nave and also as a backing for the return choir stalls.

REREDOS. Structure behind and above an altar.

RESPOND. Half-pier bonded into a wall and carrying one end of an arch.

RETICULAR. Reticulated tracery in a window typical of the early 14th century consisting entirely of circles drawn at top and bottom into ogee shapes so that a net-like appearance results.

SEDILIA. Seats for the priests on the south side of the chancel of a church.

SUPERMULLION. A term invented by Edward Augustus Freeman (1823-1892) for the multiplication of mullions in Perpendicular tracery rising from the heads of the individual lights, and forming a grid pattern (more common east of Oxford) as opposed to the 'Alternate' form which does not have supermullions continuing the line of a main mullion: instead the supermullions alternate.

TIERCERON. Secondary rib in a vault, that is, a rib which issues from one of the main springers or the central boss and leads to a place on a ridge — rib. Introduced in the early 13th century.

TRACERY. Intersecting ribwork on the upper part of a window, or used decoratively in blank arches. Y tracery is its simplest form where the mullion branches into two forming a Y shape.

TRANSEPT. Transverse portion of a cross-shaped church.

TRANSOM. Horizontal rib or bar across the openings of a window. A supertransom is a transom above the springing level of the arch of a Gothic window. The counterpart of the supertransom is formed by horizontal bands of crossed ogees linking mullion to mullion. A lattice of X transom is not very common but is found in Gloucestershire.

TRIBUNE. Upper storey above an aisle, opened in arches to the nave or chancel.

TRIFORIUM. Arcaded wall passage facing the nave at the height of the aisle roof and below the clerestorey windows.

VAULT. Continuous arched stone roof or a series of arches whose ribs radiate from a central springing point or line.

VOLUTE CAPITAL. The head or top part of a column with a spiral scroll, originally one of the component parts of an Ionic capital.

WALL PLATE. Timber or course laid horizontally on top of a wall.

INDEX